CHANNELING THE MOTHERSHIP

Published by Wisdom House Books, Inc.

Chapel Hill, North Carolina 27514 USA | 1.919.883.4669 | www.wisdomhousebooks.com

Wisdom House Books is committed to excellence in the publishing industry.

Cover and Interior design by Ted Ruybal

Published in the United States of America

Paperback ISBN: 978-0-99882610-3

LCCN: 2017952760

1. OCC003000 BODY, MIND & SPIRIT / Channeling & Mediumship

2. OCC007000 BODY, MIND & SPIRIT / Parapsychology / ESP (Clairvoyance, Precognition, Telepathy)

First Edition

14 13 12 11 10 / 10 9 8 7 6 5 4 3 2 1

CHAN

TH

MOTHERSHIP

CHANNELING THE MOTHERSHIP

Messages from the Universe

JERRY MCDANIEL
Psychic Medium and Clairvoyant

2017

DEDICATION

This book is dedicated with love and light to the following:

God/Universe/Spirit

From the above everything flows . . .

Jesus/Mary Blessed Mother/Buddha

The greatest teachers of the highest on high . . . compassion, love, and wisdom.

My Wife, Partner, and Soul Mate

Mary . . . without her, this journey would have no substance, purpose, or life. She is my reason for being.

My Children

Katie, Patrick, and Andrew, and their significant others, are the greatest kids in the world, whom I'm indebted to forever for making me so proud.

My Grandchildren

Quinn and Kellan bring a smile to my face even during the darkest times. They are a joy to me and give me hope for the future.

The Pulse Victims

To the forty-nine victims of the Pulse nightclub shooting in Orlando. Their spirits and souls live on.

Cyndi

Who is finally sailing.

ACKNOWLEDGMENTS

The below have made this book possible . . . I will never be able to repay the debt. I love you all.

Caroline, Saleen, Msgr Morris, Sam, Mark, The Gypsy Lady, and all of my Spirit Guides and Helpers who waited patiently for me to wake up from my slumber. (And Seraphina.)

Sunday Evening Medium Meditation Circle to this day remains one of the finest educational, spiritual, and knowledgeable environments I've ever been a part of.

Annette who introduced Mary and I to the world of mediumship that has helped to define our lives.

Emilio who is simply one of the Holiest men I've ever met . . . the best teacher and leader that a person can ever hope to learn from and then call friend.

Spiritual Church of Awareness: Thanks for letting an 'honorary' Spiritualist speak during Wednesday evening services.

Saturday Morning Prayer Group: This group that I've been a part of for over thirty years gives me oxygen to live and strive to be a better person.

The Planet Company: Thanks for a great career and for allowing me to gracefully exit so I can pursue God's work.

Oracle of the Age Group: A year spent with this group made me wiser, more open to my psychic gifts, and created friends for life.

The People That I've Been Privileged to Give Readings: Thank you for allowing Spirit to work through me, to hopefully give you a glimpse of the greatness that the Universe has placed inside of you.

St. Stephens Catholic Community: Thank you for being a place where all are welcome.

My Higher Self: Thanks to you, I finally woke up.

TABLE OF CONTENTS

FOREWORD

The thoughts in this book express the thoughts of a man who has worked hard towards developing his latent spiritual gifts. The driving force behind his efforts is his sincere desire to help his fellow man. The messages contained in this book are his way to bring to the foreground a unique way of looking and contemplating the world from a spiritual and metaphysical point of view.

In his search to better himself, although he is a devout Catholic, he has attended spiritual conferences, practiced daily meditation, taken mediumship classes, and has sat in a development circle. I believe it was in the mediumship development/meditation group that he acquired the insight to his spiritual gifts and an understanding of spirit communication, which he uses to help inspire other people along their path.

Channeling the Mothership is a project that was inspired by his guides, many of which are from the cloth. Many of these guides have religious backgrounds and are from all ways of life. I know that these messages are not meant to be of any one religion but one of a spiritual foundation that is all inclusive.

Emilio Lebron
Spiritualist Teacher, Author, Lecturer and Healer

Praise for *Channeling the Mothership*

Through exploration of his higher purpose and innate desire to serve others, Jerry has intuitively captured in these pages how you can acknowledge your greatness and transform your life. If you are open and willing to take a step forward, you will receive boundless clarity and direction in a way that only he can provide.

Using his mediumship gifts, he shares perspective and actionable steps for your consideration. His pure intentions to provide tremendous value and the possibility for growth are evident. Each chapter will take you on a journey that you will want to revisit time and again.

Channeling the Mothership is an act of love for all souls. I encourage you to use the words, thoughts, and messages enclosed with great excitement! This is the book to share with others. It is not only my honor to call Jerry a true friend, but to highly recommend his work, as well. Be prepared to receive and be delighted!

Elizabeth Gifford Maffei
Intuitive Business Coach, Speaker, Author, & Healer

Jerry is a master at conveying that which is deeply meaningful, the stuff that transformation is made of. This particular kind of information deserves both pause and a measure of your undivided attention, which you will find in *Channeling the Mothership*.

It will stretch you and ask only that you consider its possibility. Jerry speaks the language of the soul; he has the ability to access a universal line of energy that I call the Truth. The Big Sparkly.

It is clean in the most important ways, free from any agenda, utterly unbiased, generative and offered humbly in service–all of which earns my highest compliment and heart-felt recommendation.

Colette Pellissier
Chief Evolution Officer, Illuminated Leadership

Jerry has offered guidance and support for so many individuals. He says it best in one of his messages, "It's time to unshackle the chains that have bound you. . . ." Personally, I find this to be so helpful, and I can only imagine how many other people for whom this has provided a sense of relief and a new sense of purpose for the future. *Channeling the Mothership* will provide this relief and purpose for you, if you're open to it.

1 Corinthians 12:4 states this . . . "There are different kinds of gifts but the same Spirit distributes them. There are different kinds of service, but the same Lord. There are different kinds of working, but in all of them and in everyone it is the same God at work."

Jerry has developed his God-given gift in such a way that has helped numerous others.

Dr. Christie Cooper
President, Cooper Consulting Group

INTRODUCTION

My name is Jerry McDaniel, and I'm a psychic medium and clairvoyant. I channel the Universe. You may have no earthly idea of what that means, and that's okay. Here's what I perceive the Universe to be and how one goes about "channeling" it:

The Universe is a living, breathing entity all its own, and then again, not all its own. That's about as clear as mud, but let me explain further.

The Universe has a feminine quality of nurturing, caring, and unconditional love. So, to me the Universe is the ultimate Mothership. The Universe is in, around, and through everything and everyone.

I received messages from the Universe, from God, and from the Spirit world and put them into this book. This book is designed to get you to think and to push beyond the boundaries in your life, to meditate and reflect on your purpose and mission on the path you are on. *Channeling the Mothership* is based on what I call "Spiritual Metaphysics."

What started out as the *Channeling the Mothership* blog that I wrote for two years, transformed through inspiration, writings, and messages from the Universe into the book that you are now holding in your hand.

So, where does the Universe fit into the grand scheme of things? Technically, it is the grand scheme of things with three key interchangeable parts.

Three things make up what I call the "Metaphysical Triangle": God, the Universe, and Spirit. They are all interchangeable.

Confusing? I know. Think of it this way: No matter who you are, you are several things rolled up into one.

Me? I'm a father, son, brother, uncle, grandfather, friend, co-worker, psychic medium, clairvoyant, etc.

But I'm still Jerry Patrick McDaniel. So it is with the Metaphysical Triangle. The three components of this triangle work together in harmony.

So, what exactly is channeling?

Channeling is a form of communication or conduit with and/or between people, places, and things (which could be energy) that are not of this physical world. It could be of a psychic nature, which means reading vibrations of this world and passing along messages for people who are on a certain path in order to give them advice and counsel. It could be of a mediumship nature by receiving messages from loved ones who have passed. It could be receiving messages from our Spirit Guides, to pass along to people who truly need some help. It could be of a clairvoyant nature, whereby images, pictures, symbols, future events, etcetera are seen.

Channeling could involve energy, light, vibrations . . . the list could be endless. All I know is everything is connected with the Universe, and the Universe itself is of a metaphysical and spiritual nature.

Spirit Guides are beings of light who once walked the earth, and you have had numerous and various Spirit Guides with you throughout your life. You may know a few of them, but most of them you will not know, because they could be several hundred years old. They are here for you. It is a great time to get acquainted with them by starting to talk to them. They will reveal themselves to you once you start the conversation.

Here are a few notes about this book:

Seven Chapters: One evening, it was revealed to me that there are seven veils or pathways that need to be parted in order to reach a higher understanding. These pathways are: ENLIGHTENMENT, COURAGE, WISDOM, SILENCE, DISCOVERY, HOPE, and GRACE.

Forty-nine Messages: Why forty-nine messages? I heard a voice that said, "Stop at forty-nine." It didn't seem to make sense to me, until I investigated the number and found it to be a very spiritual number. The number "forty-nine" is prominent in numerous religions. It was the age of the Blessed Virgin when Jesus made his Ascension. The forty-ninth angel signifies that the Spirit Guides are signaling the end of a venture or series of events. The last reason that came to me in an "aha" moment long after I had stopped at forty-nine, was to pay respect to the forty-nine souls who lost their lives at the horrific mass shooting at the Pulse nightclub in Orlando, Florida in 2016.

The Universe asks three things of you as you read this book:

Navigating the Messages: Firstly, just like you would in any Universe, you will have to do some navigating. So, at the end of each of the forty-nine messages, there's going to be a few thoughts on navigating through the message that may be helpful to you.

Creating Space for Reflection: Secondly, create some space for yourself to reflect upon the message. Time and space are things we seem to find in short supply. You owe it to yourself.

Moving Forward: Thirdly, use the navigation and the reflection to take a step or two and put the message into action.

As you read this book, see which messages speak to you and why. Sit down and relax, but be sure to buckle up. It is time to begin your journey where the Universe will be looking for passengers to become participants. The question is: Are you ready to come aboard the Mothership? Time to turn the page and find out.

Chapter 1

ENLIGHTENMENT

Metaphysical vs. Spiritual

I can hear it now, "Jerry speaks with the dead. He's sleeping with the devil because you shouldn't talk to the deceased." "Whatever Jerry's doing, it's not being a Christian." "I cannot believe Jerry is calling upon those that have passed." "Just look at Jerry's Facebook page . . . he's into that New Age religion!" (That one was actually said about me.) People are usually afraid of what they do not understand or comprehend. And gifts from God are no exception.

Firstly, I do not talk to the deceased–they talk to me. Sometimes, but not all the time. Secondly, I have no idea what a New Age religion looks like. Thirdly, I'm Catholic and go to mass, and I haven't burned yet, nor do I plan on it. Fourthly, great idea. Please go to my Facebook page, @jmacmedium. Fifthly, my gifts have brought me closer to God than I have ever been before. So, to me that's not treading on sacred ground; That's actually plowing more sacred ground for people to find their true mission and purpose in life. That's my quest.

When we talk to the Universe, to the Mothership, are we breaking any rules? Is there forbidden or sacred ground that we step upon when we contact Spirit?

Are these gifts metaphysical or spiritual in nature? They're both. The way I see it is Spiritual Metaphysics. That's about the best way I can describe my gifts.

When we say that we can channel our Higher Self, that we can channel Spirit, or that we can reach others on the "other side," are we doing the work of the dark and evil?

In short, no. We're doing the work of the beloved. I'm convinced now more than ever that the gifts of prophecy, psychic, mediumship, and clairvoyance are not only God-inspired, but also, in truth and reality, much needed in the world today.

What most people forget is that God gives us free will; we have the ability to change the course of our lives and the course of our destiny and the course of others that we surround ourselves with.

No gift can predict the future with 100% certainty. If it does, it's not a gift from God.

NAVIGATING THE MESSAGE—Communicating with the Universe is actually doing the work of the Divine. Some of the most gratifying experiences I've ever had were helping others to make better decisions, to heal, and to move on with their spiritual path in life.

CREATING SPACE FOR REFLECTION—Consider this for a moment. Is God a puppet-master pulling strings so that we have to wait to hear from Him before we make any moves or make any decisions? I think you know the answer to that one. No, of course not, because that's not how love works. We're given gifts, but it's up to us to use them. So, meditate on what gifts you have, and if you're not sure, ask the Universe. Rely upon your intuition—that small still voice inside your head—to help you with your questions on your gifts.

MOVING FORWARD—Time to put your gifts to use. Gifts are meant to be shared, not held onto. There is someone who is in need, and I'm sure you know whom it is. Time to help that person who could really use your talents. And guess what . . . behind that person is not only more people who need your gifts, but also people who will use their gifts to help you, no strings attached.

A Bath Becomes a Sanctuary for the Calling

I always wanted to be a jogger. So I took up jogging around the age of thirty-five, and, over the years, I worked my way up to running twenty-five miles a week. I did very well for a number of years, slowly but surely improving my time, until two back surgeries took me down a few ego notches and forced me to take up walking instead.

To ease my occasional pains before and after walking, I would take a long, hot bath, to loosen my back. I would close my eyes, ease into the tub, and relax. But for years, something kept happening that I could not explain. When I closed my eyes, I would see images, pictures, and scenes that seemed to be out of a movie. It was a movie that I had never seen, with people that I had never met and places that I had never been.

I thought that I must have fallen asleep and was simply dreaming, but then I would hear a plane go overhead, or kids playing outside our house, or the TV in our living room. I saw these images and pictures with my eyes closed, but I was not dreaming.

I have ADD, but seeing these images was beyond that. I began to notice other strange happenings around me. Several times a day, someone would say something that I had been thinking right before they said it. I would hear voices and noises that seemed to come out of nowhere. They were small, subtle voices and noises that no one heard and that I never paid attention to. They now seemed to be wanting my attention, but why?

One day, I had a chance encounter with a lady who came to clean our house who was more than just a cleaning lady. Her name was Annette, and she casually said one day that she was a medium. I had heard of mediums before but never gave them much notice. She said she could give me a reading after she was through cleaning our house. I was intrigued and said yes.

When we sat down to talk, she went into specific detail about my grandfather, of which there weren't any pictures in the house. I was intrigued and soon afterwards, so was my wife. She introduced us both to the weekly medium meditation circle that she attended, and the rest is history. I wanted to be of service to people using these newfound gifts that I was developing. I had found my calling.

She told me, "Jerry, once you decide to open this door in your life, Spirit will work with you more and more. When you open more doors and open yourself to Spirit, more will be given to you and more will be expected of you." Since then I've become a psychic medium and clairvoyant, performed readings internationally for people of all walks of life, and, along the way, I obtained various certifications.

It was time to get serious, to fulfill my destiny during this lifetime, and help people not only move on with life, but reach down and help them to pull out their deepest desires, dreams, goals, and aspirations to see the potential that lies within and help them see that they, too, have a responsibility and a calling to help people. We're all in this together.

NAVIGATING THE MESSAGE—We all have a calling in our lives. We need to be prepared for the calling that might come out of nowhere, at a place and time when we least expect it.

CREATING SPACE FOR REFLECTION—Take time to ask yourself: What calling have you experienced? Heard? Ignored? Postponed? Rejected? More importantly . . . why?

MOVING FORWARD—Pay attention to the seemingly random thoughts and activities that occur in your life on a day-to-day basis. Nothing is random, as it all connects like pieces in a puzzle. Soon your calling will start to take shape and reveal itself. That calling is a sacred calling and do not let anyone else convince you otherwise.

Is *The Matrix* a Reality?

One evening, I was sitting on my couch watching TV while my wife was sitting across from me in her favorite chair, reading. I happened to turn towards the kitchen just in time to catch a blue and white polka-dot dress flash in front of me. It happened so quickly that I had no idea what I had just witnessed and had zero time to even begin to comprehend what I saw. The mediums would go on to explain that this was simply one person traveling from one dimension to another. And they told me this without me even telling them what I had witnessed.

Dimensions . . . could it be true that a person or being could travel from one dimension to another, like hopping from train to train?

As strange and surreal as it sounds, I have found more and more folks who are ardent supporters of the idea that the Universe, metaphysically and spiritually, is comprised of several levels and layers of dimensions. The higher the dimension, the higher the vibrations and light a person will go through and obtain.

There are numerous dimensions in this Universe.

In the 1999 movie *The Matrix*,[1] the Wachowski sisters presented us with an image of our world as an imaginary place created as a facade by a cyber intelligence. So, is the world we live in just a façade? What is real and what isn't?

Is this all there is to life? We play, go to school, work, fall in love, perhaps raise a family . . . then what?

That's it? Then we die, and what? This cannot be all there is . . . right?

As you go about your daily life, don't you wonder what else is out there?

I've asked the question often: Why do we look up? Are we looking for something more out of life? And not knowing where to look, do we look up to God, to the Universe, to Spirit, or as I say, to the Mothership?

I do believe that the life we are currently living is like the tip of the iceberg . . . only 10-15% is shown above the water and the rest is below the surface, waiting to be discovered. However, icebergs eventually melt.

NAVIGATING THE MESSAGE—The Universe teaches us that there is more to life . . . to knowledge . . . to discovering more of who we are and what our purpose and mission in life is.

Richard Rohr tells us that this is part of the second half of life . . . a half that hopefully starts to show us what this life *is* all or *should* be all about.

CREATING SPACE FOR REFLECTION—Imagine yourself at a pot-luck dinner; you know, those dinners where everyone brings something of value to share. Now imagine you've been invited to come to a pot luck dream gathering at which people from all walks of life will not bring food to share, but will bring their dreams, goals, desires, ambitions, mission, purpose, etc. to share.

What will you bring to this gathering? Take five minutes and ask yourself . . . "What do I really want to do in life?"

MOVING FORWARD—Now, write down your answers.

Make a vision Post-it note. It's a start. But, don't let it be the tip of the iceberg because there's more where that came from submerged beneath the water. It's time to surface. Now, get going because dinner is almost ready.

The Death of One's Ego Gives Birth to Enlightenment

The Universe is all about enlightenment. That's how we learn, that's how we evolve, and that's how we move forward with our life. And the more we move forward with our life, the closer we come to learning what is important in life and what is not. The Universe knows that there are roadblocks set up, mainly by ourselves, that prevent us from realizing our full potential.

One of the biggest roadblocks is ego. Ego tells us that we have to win at everything in life, and if we don't win, then there's going to be consequences. We're going to have to try harder and put more effort in beating our fellow man and woman in how we look, how smart we are, how nice our car or house is, how much better we are at our jobs, how much money we make, how our kids are better than anyone else's, how nice our yard is compared to that of our neighbors', and, and, and. The Universe knows that ego drains us of energy, and, without energy, the soul gets tired. If the soul gets tired, the Universe cannot continue to grow and evolve and expand.

The struggle with ego is real, and at times it overwhelms us. Ego divides us as a person, as a society, and as a culture. It creates conflict; it hides us from the truth; it tells us lies; it destroys friendships and creates false ones.

It tells us that we're too good for everyone else.

Ego keeps us from wondering what is on the other side. It keeps us on our one safe side saying, "We're too good to see what is on the other side," or, "Nothing to learn from them, so no need to try."

Ego's cousin, Pride, is never far behind . . . lurking in the shadows. Pride wrapped up in the false security blanket of ego never lets a person experience true freedom. Pride creates walls, borders, and boundaries. Ego reinforces them.

I've prayed for God to help me arrange the death of my ego. When you have gifts that are somewhat different than others' gifts, you begin to believe that you're really something special, that no one is truly as gifted as you, and that you're absolutely the best at what you do. You begin to believe that your gifts are better than anyone else's gifts. Nothing could be further from the truth.

I struggle with this and ask the Universe to please help me with my fantasy-driven, egocentric desires.

NAVIGATING THE MESSAGE—Can you live with the death of your ego? Once the death of your ego happens, there is an awakening, then comes enlightenment . . . then comes the ability to connect to the higher side of life. The possibilities will be endless.

CREATING SPACE FOR REFLECTION—Consider where and when your ego has let you down. Contemplate where your ego has offered up a façade of the real you to the outside world. Chances are, the situations that you found yourself in are due to your ego. The person you are, or the person you want to be, is not defined by your ego.

MOVING FORWARD—Write down your biggest fears about letting go of your ego. What is it about this process that scares you? The sooner you start to plan the passing of your ego, the quicker you will be on the road to enlightenment. Arrange to purchase the flowers for the funeral of your ego . . . no reason to wear black or mourn because a new awakening within you is about to see the light of day.

We Are Spirit with a Body

The famed Spiritualist lecturer and author, Marilyn Awtry,[2] said, "We are Spirit with a body . . . not a body with a Spirit." So what exactly does that mean? To a lot of us, it's hard to comprehend what it means to be a Spirit first. We are introduced to our body at a very young age, but not sure when we're first introduced to our Spirit. It is difficult to say, because how do you shake hands with your essence? This is not an easy topic of conversation, but one that needs to happen if we truly want to know our purpose and meaning in this lifetime.

We are Spirit first, a ball of energy, of Divine light. We have the imprint of the Divine within us and on us, and it is that fact which first and foremost defines us.

Our Spirit, our Soul, has the fingerprints of the Universe firmly imprinted on it.

Of course this goes back to the Bible's teaching, "We are made in the image and likeness of God," which means we are neither straight nor gay, black nor white, male nor female, liberal nor conservative–we are all Spirit.

NAVIGATING THE MESSAGE—Labels should not define us. Labels are unnecessary tools that provide structure to society. Structure that is, quite honestly, unnecessary. Spirit does not need a box to fit in . . . it is the box. A box that is open.

CREATING SPACE FOR REFLECTION—Ponder for a moment what labels have been placed upon you unfairly. Doesn't feel good, does it? Now, turn that coin over and think for a moment about the labels you have placed on others unfairly or simply on appearance alone.

MOVING FORWARD—You are a vessel of the Universe; time to put your oars in the water and set forth on your journey. The first thing you might consider doing is not to take people at face value. That's the shell you're looking at, but what is underneath is more important because that's their Spirit. The other side is waiting.

"If Everyone's Thinking Alike, Then No One's Thinking"

It's safe to say that when one possesses the gifts of psychic mediumship and clairvoyance, the conventional way of thinking is turned on its head. This way of thinking isn't like other folks', that's for sure. I'm sure you have your own special gifts that defy logical thinking, as well . . . everyone does, and that's what makes us all unique and different.

I've given a good number of readings and messages to folks, and I can tell you first hand that none of them were thinking the same thing, or even thinking alike, before, during, and after the reading.

Sure, when it comes to psychic readings, most folks want to know about finance, relationships, or health. But everyone has different ideas and different needs, and that's what I love about my gifts. There's no two readings that have been the same because there's no two people that have been the same.

If I was thinking like everyone else, I would have dismissed my gifts as just new age gobbledygook that had no place in my life. Thank God I finally listened to the Universe and made myself available to use the gifts that God gave me.

No gift is exactly the same; no one's story or life is the same; and no one's thinking is the same either. We are all different and unique, and so is our mindset and thought process.

No two mediums work the same way, and no two psychics work the same way. Metaphysically and spiritually, there are major differences in the way we think and act and use our gifts.

The title of this chapter is from a great quote credited to General George Patton. It is one of my favorite quotes about thinking, and it is a challenge to rewire our minds not to be the conformist. It's okay to be different and it's okay to think differently in business, in our home life, and in our personal spiritual journey. Not just thinking outside the box, but thinking without a box even present.

And while you're thinking, remember one thing. Your thoughts influence everything. More than actions and deeds, thoughts are powerful tools in this world. If what we think drives our beliefs, and what we believe in drives our behavior, then you can easily see the impact of our thought processes. Thought is the key that starts the engine; staying away from negative thinking can be the key that unlocks the power of positive thinking.

Negative thinking is what starts conflict, confrontations, separation, and disconnect. To disconnect, means to disengage, and we want our thinking to be engaging. We want our thinking to be unique and to inspire others to reach their goals, dreams, and aspirations.

Think of it this way . . . to think positively enables the stars to shine brightly in the Universe so others can find their path. Negative thinking dims the lights of the Universe and the lights of others' dreams.

Think, dream, and dare to be different and unique. Come to think of it, you already are.

NAVIGATING THE MESSAGE—What would you think about if you had no borders, no boundaries, just you and your imagination? The Universe wants you to go outside the lines, outside the limits, outside conventional wisdom and thinking, to explore the furthest edges of your mind.

CREATING SPACE FOR REFLECTION—God designed our minds to expand, to think, to reflect, and to contemplate. So, are we doing our part? One of the best business books I've read is *First, Break All the Rules* by Marcus Buckingham and Curt Coffman.[3]

What I learned from that book is this: business leaders learned that they had wasted time trying to push traits that weren't there onto people, and that they should have been pulling out all of the great traits that were already there. What do you have inside you that the Universe wants you to think about? How does Spirit want you to expand your mind with the gifts you have? What is it that God wants you to do with the knowledge you possess?

MOVING FORWARD—What has God left in you that needs to be pulled out? What strengths are within you that need to be fully realized in order for you to reach your potential?

Write them down and keep writing them down . . . you're going to be shocked by how many strengths you have.

If not everyone is thinking alike, then, hopefully, no one is thinking like you. Start to get rid of the negative thoughts that seem to run your life. What are you waiting for? A penny for your thoughts?

Prayer Is Not Having a Conversation with the Creator

In addition to being a psychic medium and clairvoyant, I also enjoyed a career as a salesman (even though I'm retired now), specializing in consumer-packaged goods for over thirty-five years. I've also been a corporate trainer and have trained over 3,000 people, from retail associates to line managers, sales people, territory managers, district managers, regional managers, etc.

What became apparent is that we salespeople (of which I'm one) fall into the trap of doing all the talking and very little listening. Normally, I'm not a good listener (ask Mary, my wife). So, how was I going to listen to Spirits, people who have passed, the Universe, my soul, or my intuition? It wasn't easy, but I was serious about these gifts, and the only way I was going to use them was to listen.

We're given two ears and one mouth for a reason, but we soon forget that reason, which brings me to religion. Many religions preach and teach us to pray, pray, pray.

We're taught and told to hit our knees and pray to God, and trust me, that's good advice, except for one thing. Prayer is *talking* to God, not listening.

The biggest mistake we make is thinking that praying to God is having a conversation with God. It's not. In order to have a conversation, there has to be talking AND listening.

How do we listen?

We meditate. It's that simple; meditation is listening to God.

God, the Universe, and Spirit already know what we want to talk about and what's on our mind. They just want us to listen.

NAVIGATING THE MESSAGE—The only way for us to discern what is truly on our mind, in our heart, and in our soul is to be quiet and listen. Only then can we hear the voice of God, the sound of Spirit and the will of the Universe. This is the Metaphysical Triangle.

CREATING SPACE FOR REFLECTION—There are 1,440 minutes in a day. Carving out just a few minutes to quiet ourselves and be in the present moment sounds like something that's easy to accomplish. Then why do we struggle to find the time? The remedy is to start today, to sit and just be.

MOVING FORWARD—For every minute of prayer, spend two minutes in meditation. For every minute that you spend asking God a question, spend two minutes listening to the answer. Now there's a conversation.

---

1. Pg. 7- The Matrix. (1999). Directed by L. Wachowski and L. Wachowski. Warner Brothers.
2. Pg. 11- Awtry, M. Author, Lecturer, Clairvoyant.
3. Pg. 15 - Buckingham, M. and Coffman, C. (1999). *First, Break All the Rules*. Simon & Schuster.

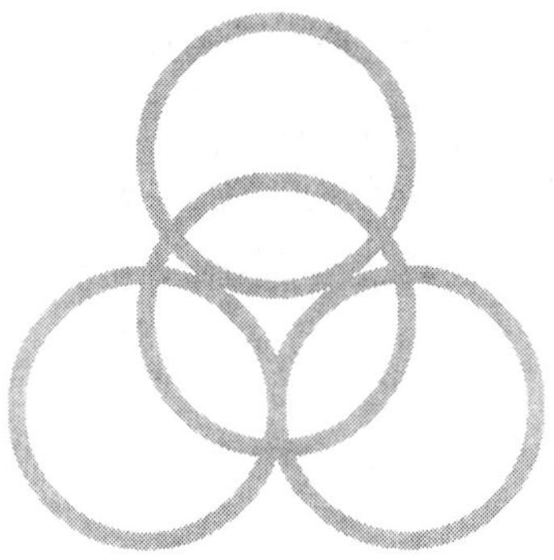

Chapter 2

COURAGE

The Story of the Girl in the Cubicle

She worked in our finance department for one or two years. I passed her cubicle numerous times, never stopping to say hello or start up a conversation. To the best of my recollection, I never met her; or, if I did, it wasn't memorable.

How many times have we done that? Passed someone without even taking the time to get to know them? I know . . . there's always tomorrow, right? The Universe never passes anyone by, but, boy do we. Think about it, every day that we spend on this earth, plane will never repeat itself, and the overwhelming majority of people we come in contact with, we will never, ever see again. Onto to the title of this chapter and, hopefully, the lesson we will all learn.

The person whom I'm referring to from that cubicle is Stephanie, and unfortunately there will not be a "tomorrow" for me to get to know her.

Stephanie and her husband, Justin, were killed in the Brussels Airport terrorist attack on March 22, 2016. From what I know, they were waving goodbye to a relative who had passed through security, and, in the blink of an eye and a flash of light, they were gone.

It was amazing that all of the comments from her co-workers spoke to Stephanie's character. They never referred to her work. They never referred to what a great job she did or how her projects were always finished on time, etc.

Instead, they talk about her smile . . . her energy . . . her spirit. That's her, (and Justin's) legacy.

Her spirit . . . her soul . . . that's what lives on, not the shell of a body that she occupied, but her pure essence lives in those who knew her best.

When a person dies, passes on, transitions, or crosses over, their soul lives on. The soul, the spirit, the light, and the energy never die. Your soul is oxygen for the Universe.

So, what did we do? We mourned, we grieved, and we moved on because that's what we do in order to carry on our legacies, our energy, light, and spirit.

We light a candle for those that we miss and for those that have lost their way and need to see the light. Tonight, light a candle for Stephanie and Justin, for those who are victims of terrorism worldwide, and for the Belgian people. Say a prayer when you light the candle. Light attracts light.

NAVIGATING THE MESSAGE—Stephanie and Justin's spirit will be felt by those who were close to them. Their lives will live on in the work that we all do on a daily basis. The Universe isn't focused on the work of our careers, but our work for humanity. If that's the case, isn't it time for us to be human and reach out to get to know the people around us?

We could all use a new spirit boost every now and then.

CREATING SPACE FOR REFLECTION—Lighting candles is one of the most sacred acts you can perform. Light attracts light. Lighting candles sends a signal to the Universe, and sometimes it sends a distress call. It sometimes pays homage to our ancestors, and sometimes it prepares us to have a conversation with Spirit.

MOVING FORWARD—Make it a goal to stop by that person in the cubicle that you've never gotten to know and say hi and start a conversation. Who knows when and where your next best friend will show up? There is no time like the present to be present to those around you and start a conversation by just saying hi.

Climbing the Decision Tree

Decisions are difficult, and the multitude of decisions that we must all face every day feels like we're climbing a huge tree. Every limb gets higher and higher, weaker and weaker, so that when we do climb out on a limb to make an important and difficult decision, the limb's almost give way to the enormous weight and pressure that is on us.

In every person's life, there is a decision that must be made . . . a big decision that is put off many times. The question is why. What is it that we're afraid of?

What guidance or reassurance do we need in order to make this big decision? Who do we call upon to give us comfort when we face the decision?

When I give readings, it is amazing what decisions–important, impactful decisions–need to be made that have yet to be made. The people in front of me receiving the reading are sometimes absolutely petrified. We are so afraid of making a mistake that we live our lives in fear. We are paralyzed with indecision.

The Universe knows it, your soul knows it, Spirit knows it, God knows it, and, of course, you know it.

Until we decide, the Universe cannot help or guide us. The Universe is powerless to act, and, in this powerlessness, it cannot help keep us on the path to enlightenment. The Universe is around us, in us, and through us. The Universe is God, and God is the Universe. But the Universe will never circumvent the free will that is given to us by the Divine. The Universe will never make the decision for you, which brings us to the burning question . . . why haven't you made the decision? Time is of the essence.

NAVIGATING THE MESSAGE—Procrastination is not the way to go, trust me, I know. Putting off a major decision will mean a huge missed opportunity that may never ever come again.

CREATING SPACE FOR REFLECTION—Think about it; something that could make a difference in your life, or, more importantly, put you on a better and more enlightening path, is within your grasp. Think about what decision or decisions you may have already set aside. Have a conversation within yourself to take the plunge and go forward.

MOVING FORWARD—Take a deep breath; reach deep down within yourself and make that decision. It's not going away. The result that you have been struggling with is right in front of you.

Stop dreaming. Wake up or, better yet, go climb a tree.

Mystical Musical Chairs

First of all, what is a mystic? Because if we don't know what a mystic is, how can we know that we're being called to be one? Here's an abbreviated definition of a mystic: "a person who seeks by contemplation and self-surrender to obtain unity with the Deity or the absolute" (Oxford Dictionaries)[1].

Pretty heavy stuff, huh? I'm sure the typical to-do list doesn't read like this:

- FINISH THE PROJECT AT WORK
- PICK UP MILK AND BREAD
- WORK WITH THE KIDS ON THEIR HOMEWORK
- CUT THE GRASS
- ANSWER THE CALL TO BE A MYSTIC

If it does, then why in the world are you even reading this book? Let's be honest, this is way above our heads–or is it? Let's look at three key words in the definition that might help us:

CONTEMPLATION, SELF-SURRENDER, and UNITY.

To be honest, those three words describe my readings as a psychic, medium, and clairvoyant. Before I begin my readings, I pray and contemplate about the reading and the person that I'm about to speak to.

During the reading, I try my best to surrender myself to the Universe, so that I can achieve unity and give the best messages to the person in front of me.

But don't you do the same? I believe you do, but you may not realize it. Your intuition will help you with these three key words.

When does your intuition tell you to self-surrender? More importantly, *what* does your intuition tell you to self-surrender? When does your intuition tell you that there's something bigger than yourself and that "something bigger" wants to draw closer to you?

Contemplation calls us to think deeply . . . even Atheists (notice out of respect I capitalized the "A") think deeply, and, in fact, Atheists have a deep belief system even in the things they don't believe. To contemplate, simply means to think about something, hopefully of a spiritual nature, for an extended period of time.

And unity . . . don't we all attempt to achieve unity and become one when we pray or meditate or ask questions of our creator? Are we yearning to draw closer with the Universe and draw closer to God? To me, that's seeking unity in a nutshell. The mystics of years ago realized that, in contemplation, they could attempt to seek union with God and live that life in harmonious relationship with the Universe.

Their beliefs drove their behavior.

What beliefs do you have that cause you to think, act, and behave the way you do? Is it seeking unity with the Divine? Is it rooted in love? Does it cause you to want to be a better person today than you were yesterday? A better person tomorrow than you were today?

NAVIGATING THE MESSAGE—Mystics didn't just believe in contemplation, they lived it. They breathed it. It was like oxygen to them, and they couldn't get enough of it.

CREATING SPACE FOR REFLECTION—Are you being called to be a modern-day mystic? Do you covet a union with God? Is a deeper relationship with and understanding of the Universe what drives you?

MOVING FORWARD—Do you want to be one with Spirit? Don't strain to hear God or attempt to get His attention . . . just close your eyes and listen.

Pioneering the New Frontier

I never thought much about psychic abilities, mediumship, or clairvoyance. I didn't give any thoughts to connecting to the Spirit world. To me, it was all mumbo jumbo and meant for someone else. I'm not sure if I ever believed in connecting to the other side. Oh, sure, I had heard of psychics predicting the future and mediums talking to people who had died, but I never gave it one minute of thought. I was comfortable in my own world, doing my own daily routines, and I didn't need anybody or anything upsetting my apple cart.

Then one day in the weekly medium circle, I was asked to give a message to the person sitting in front of me. To my surprise, I delivered a couple of messages and received validations almost immediately. A New Frontier was waiting for me. I opened the door, and life hasn't been the same for me since. What exactly is the New Frontier and, more importantly, where is it?

Only your mind, your soul, and your imagination know what and where the New Frontier is.

To me, it's the Universe. And the Universe needs to be explored, needs to be examined, needs to be prayed on, around and through. The Universe needs to continue to expand, and you're going to have to pioneer that frontier. Think of it this way, if you're going to continue to learn, evolve, and improve your life, the current status quo isn't going to cut it.

During the readings that I have been honored to give to people, it is so gratifying when the Universe reaches down and pulls out something to explore, something to contemplate, something to seriously ponder from deep in their soul, sometimes buried for years and years because of neglect. Yes. It is a New Frontier, and it's been waiting to be awakened.

So, what is it that you haven't explored, examined, or thought about? Perhaps you've dismissed something with a casual brush aside, or haven't wondered about, pondered on, meditated, or contemplated? In perhaps . . . forever?

The New Frontier is something that is on the horizon, something that is in the distance. It is something that yearns for us to go and explore and question and inquire about.

Your mind, soul, and imagination know no boundaries, and so in that respect, the New Frontier is internal as much as it is external.

Here's a question for you and for us all . . . how can we learn from those whom we have judged for so long?

NAVIGATING THE MESSAGE—We all judge. It seems to be a part of our human DNA, but what if . . . just what if we sat down and attempted to learn at least one thing from someone or something that we have judged, either closely or from afar? What would be the result of that action? Only a pioneer brave enough to tackle that assignment would dare to open that door and step in. That's the kind of frontier that I'm talking about.

CREATING SPACE FOR REFLECTION—As I said earlier, I didn't think much about psychic abilities, mediumship, or clairvoyance until that fateful day that I opened the door and walked in. My life hasn't been the same since, and neither will yours if you take a chance and be that pioneer that the Universe is calling you to be. For that day, I am grateful and still eager to push the boundaries of any new frontiers that are waiting to be discovered.

MOVING FORWARD—There are other borders to cross and explore, but only if you have what it takes to be a pioneer and open that door.

Look around . . . what needs to be changed in this world? What gifts and talents do you have to enact the change that is so desperately needed? All it takes is one act to start the process. So, do you have what it takes? Only you can answer that question.

Welcome to the Courtyard of Opposite Thinking

I know a thing or two about people who think the exact opposite as me, and, I'm sure, so do you.

When you decide to step out and proclaim gifts such as mediumship, psychic abilities, and clairvoyance, people are going to stare at you, talk behind your back, point at you, and even make comments about you. It's taking "opposite thinking" to an entirely new level.

I even had someone, whom I thought was a good friend, talk to an elder at my church and tell him that I was into "new age" religion and questioned my "new direction."

As I've mentioned before, the Catholic Church doesn't exactly embrace these gifts, but Spirit has told me that one of the main purposes for my gifts is to reach out to people in my Catholic faith and demonstrate that these gifts are truly from God.

The Universe allows all sorts of thinking because the Universe includes everything and everybody, and it excludes no one. It includes people who have the exact opposite mindset that we possess.

How does that make us feel?

If you had a way to bridge that gap in the mindsets, would you take that opportunity? Very few people would.

Try this . . . close your eyes and try to imagine yourself on the banks of a river. Across the way could be people who do not think as you do. They do not dress as you do. They don't share the same political views. They are complete opposites of you and what you stand for. They are the very people that you have avoided most.

These are people that perhaps you have judged, and who knows, maybe they have judged you, as well.

NAVIGATING THE MESSAGE—It is time to put an end to all of the judgement. If you decide to go across the water, there will be two sets of doors that lead into a courtyard for you to enter.

CREATING SPACE FOR REFLECTION—If you choose to open the doors, in this courtyard will be people who are direct opposites of you; some you may even know.

Many people before you have chosen not to enter the water, much less get to the other side and open the doors. They never entered the courtyard and started the conversation. Keep in mind that YOU are the complete opposite of them.

MOVING FORWARD—Open the doors, enter the courtyard and at least start the conversation. See what the fuss was all about that made you want to separate yourself from them. Listen to them and see what they think, say, and do. Remember, the Universe looks after them as much as the Universe looks after you. Communicate and keep the conversation going.

Start to make a change. One final question . . . how hard will you try to make it to the other side? You'll never know unless . . .

Living on the Edge of Expectations

Life is full of expectations. Trust me, I know. As a psychic medium, I'm expected to know everything about everything and everybody, with zero margin for error. After all, I have these gifts, so people expect me to be perfect in them, even though none of them (or you or I) are perfect in anything we do. Some people have certain expectations when it comes to readings, and I'm aware of this even before the reading begins. But there is a catch.

As a clairvoyant, I'm expected to know what each little symbol that I see means and, in addition to that, what that symbol means to the person or group receiving the reading(s). Living up to others' expectations is a burden that I firmly believe we all carry.

The minute I don't live up to others' expectations of what my gifts should be in their opinion, I'm labeled ineffective, or a fake, or phony, or worse. Labels have expectations tied to them, and my gifts are no exception. You see, society needs expectations to fill in the blanks . . . to fill the gap where structure doesn't quite fit the bill. We expect so much of others and, at times, so little of ourselves.

Don't get me wrong . . . we have to be citizens of the world and contributing members of society. But that doesn't mean we have to contribute all of our dreams, wants, and desires that no one else sees in order to fulfill society's demands and expectations.

We're actually living on the edge of expectations . . . why? Because it's what life expects of us . . . we have to live up to everyone else's expectations of who we are . . . how we live our lives . . . and what kind of people we are in order to fit in and please everyone.

What would happen if we didn't have to live up to everyone's expectations? It's time to ask our souls in silent contemplation, "I've grown tired of society's expectations. Now it's time to fulfill my destiny, whatever that destiny is." What a great question to want an answer to!

NAVIGATING THE MESSAGE—Spirit reaches into the soul, pulls out those desires that have been buried because of society's expectations, and brings them to the surface to breathe once again.

CREATING SPACE FOR REFLECTION—The look on people's faces when they realize that there are endless possibilities within them that are crying out for air is priceless. It's unreal to see the joy on people's faces when they realize not all is lost, that there is more to come in this lifetime in order to fulfill the soul's desires and achieve happiness.

MOVING FORWARD—Boundaries are a good thing. It's tough to live up to everyone's expectations when sometimes we don't live up to our own expectations. Do you allow people to invade your boundaries, your space, your borders of what is acceptable and what isn't? Do you constantly say, "I really wish they wouldn't do that?" And they continue to do it time and time again. Time to set some boundaries, for you do not have to give people permission to define what your expectations should or shouldn't be. I say throw away everyone's expectations of you, and live the life you were meant to live. It's time to jump off the edge of expectations. No need to worry about the surface below you; with no expectations to live up to, you may never land.

A Boat, a Plane, and a Helicopter

It's the old joke, right?

A gentlemen is on top of his house in the midst of a flood and waves off a boat, saying, "God will save me." Then he waves off a plane, saying again, "God will save me." Then he waves off a helicopter, saying again, "God will save me."

The water rises too high, and the man drowns. In Heaven, he asks God "Why didn't you save me?"

God sighs and says, "Are you kidding me? I sent you a boat and a plane and a helicopter."

By now you're laughing I'm sure, but life is like that. There are signs all around us, some literal and some symbolic. Everything around us means something.

As a clairvoyant, I see signs that pop up in readings all the time.

It's up to the person receiving the symbols and signs to interpret them. I can only interpret what the Universe wants me to interpret. It's not always easy; but eventually the universe will reveal itself through these signs.

For months, I was giving readings to a number of people, and I found myself at a most curious crossroads. It seemed like at certain times during some of these readings, I was making the same exact points . . . over and over again. I would catch myself thinking, "What in the world is going on? Didn't I just say that exact same thing the other day?"

These points were actually laying out a path for me to start my own blog, the one that served as the foundation for this book. The Universe was giving me messages through the readings that I was giving to other people. The messages were serving a dual purpose, but I finally connected the dots on the signs that I was receiving.

Some signs are meant to impact us immediately, and some are seeds that are planted in our soul, to be revealed and interpreted at a later date. We're not meant to know everything right now. Next time you're out for a drive, look around and see what signs are being placed in front of you. Try to make meanings for what you observe.

For example, you look at a clock and it indicates a certain time. Does that time reflect someone's birthday? Anniversary? Someone's passing? Or perhaps a clue to something even bigger?

This one never ceases to amaze me. You're at a stop light. Look at the license plate in front of you. Does it have a special meaning to you? The numbers? The letters? The state? You're going to be blown away by how the Universe attempts to get our attention and communicate with us.

It's all around us. Everywhere we look are chapters in the Universal book that need to be read. All we have to do is turn the page.

NAVIGATING THE MESSAGE—During readings, we have to be a willing participant. By working and discerning the symbols and signs, we become a partner with the Universe in discovering the true message(s) of the reading.

The most unusual signs appear to us in the most unlikely of places. That's the beauty of the Universe.

CREATING SPACE FOR REFLECTION—Look at your refrigerator . . . I'm sure there are tons of magnets holding notes, telephone numbers, flyers, reminders, etc. As you go to the refrigerator to get some food or a drink, the magnets are meant to get your attention. That's a part of your Universe, and it's no different than going through your day and observing the signs that the Universe puts in front of you, to get your attention.

MOVING FORWARD—What signs have you noticed that seem to repeat themselves? What signs have you noticed that seem out of place? Now, what do you do with that information? Let me know if you happen to see a boat, a plane, or a helicopter.

1. Pg. 24 - Oxford Dictionaries. (2017). Oxford Dictionaries | Our story, products, technology, and news. [online] Available at: http://Oxforddictionaries.com.

Chapter 3

WISDOM

Connecting the Dots on Quantum Entanglement

When people who have passed make contact with me to pass along messages to loved ones, it reinforces to me that we are all connected, both among the living and those that are in the Spirit world. When I was introduced to my Spirit guides by mediums whom I met with on a weekly basis, I was amazed to learn that people from all walks of life, from all parts of the world, and from hundreds of years ago were connected to me, and I to them.

When we do something, say something, or think something, our words, actions, and thoughts have an impact on the entire world and the entire Universe. As unreal as it seems, distance is irrelevant when it comes to connections.

I was first introduced to the term "Quantum Entanglement" by Dr. Ilia Delio at a conference in 2014. It has opened my eyes with this quote that I took during her talk(s): "As human beings, we seem separate, but in our roots we are part of an indivisible whole and share in the same cosmic universe."[1]

I'm connected to everyone and everything in my state of Florida, my country of USA, my planet Earth, my Universe and beyond. As a straight, conservative Republican, this means I'm connected to a gay, liberal Democrat.

Hatred has no place in my life, and I care about the richest and the poorest. I love my Muslim brother and sister who are probably persecuted more than I realize. This is a lot to comprehend, a lot to take in, and a lot to contemplate. This is more than just thinking about things, and more than just love your brother and sister. It means love; period.

NAVIGATING THE MESSAGE—Think of Quantum Entanglement this way. What do you think of when you think of your soul? To me, your soul is oxygen for the Universe. It gives life to the Universe, and so from that aspect we're all connected because we all share in the same breath of the Divine.

CREATING THE SPACE FOR REFLECTION—So what happens when we die? Because your soul never dies, you never die. You live on, and so does the Universe. We never lose the connection between one another, and we never will. This becomes the realization that everything you do and think about has consequences for someone else in this world and this Universe.

MOVING FORWARD—As a child of the Universe, realize that you need to do better because someone somewhere is counting on you. Your thoughts, words, and actions influence others and vice versa. We're all counting on each other, but it starts with me . . . and you.

When You Close Your Eyes, What Do You See?

As I soaked in a hot bath after a 10-mile walk, I closed my eyes and saw yet another series of scenes and images of people that I did not know, in places that I was not familiar with and had never been. This had gone on for years and years, and I just assumed it was part of my ADD.

Until one day I realized something! I was not falling asleep in the tub. This was not part of my ADD . . . this was something else. It finally hit me as I heard the TV in our living room with my eyes closed and still witnessed the images, scenes, etc. that kept rolling in front of my closed eyes.

It was then that I was introduced to clairvoyance, a French word meaning clear vision or clear seeing with something that was referred to as our "Third Eye."

Seeing with our eyes closed.

The Third Eye refers to the gate that leads to inner realms and spaces of higher consciousness.

It's featured in Eastern religions, and even talked about in Catholicism by Fr. Richard Rohr,[2] who uses it as a metaphor to talk about the ability to use more than our two eyes in order to see how the mystics see, in a non-dualistic way.

My Third Eye has shown me things that have not only helped me on my spiritual journey, but have also enabled me to help others, as well.

God works in mysterious ways . . . it's one of the beauties and wonders of the Universe.

Speaking of mysterious ways and closing our eyes . . . what about our dreams? More specifically, what about *your* dreams? What are they about? What do they involve? Do they seem real?

Dreams are one of the most mysterious and magical portals to the Spirit world.

When we dream, we relax and leave the worries of the day behind. We drop our shields and borders and boundaries and the suit of armor that we used to defend ourselves from everyone who wanted a piece of us earlier in the day.

Phone calls, emails, kids crying, adults crying, people yelling and screaming, road rage, wars, politics, TVs blaring, people running from place to place and appointment to appointment as if they're in a marathon, and on and on and on it goes, day after day, week after week, month after month, year after year, and well, you get the point.

It's no wonder that Spirit attempts to contact us during this time because that's the only way that they can get our attention sometimes. It's the only way we can engage in a conversation with the Universe. Close your eyes and watch, learn, and listen.

NAVIGATING THE MESSAGE—Your dreams are a gateway to things wondrous and exciting, but only if we start to pay attention to them. Dreams . . . where we can go anywhere we want, meet anyone we want, and do anything we want, including converse with the other side.

CREATING SPACE FOR REFLECTION—If you're up for it, write down your dreams, or at least what you can remember. You will be surprised that, after several dreams, a pattern will start to form. This pattern is the Universe talking to you.

MOVING FORWARD—Tonight, when you close your eyes, before you drift off to sleep, ask Spirit to contact you somehow and in some way in your dreams . . . then grab some imaginary popcorn and enjoy the show. The Universe has something for you to see.

Is Our Free Will Just an Illusion?

I tell people during my readings about free will so much that I sound like a broken record. It's important for me to make the distinction because people need to understand the uncertainties of a reading, as it pertains to future events. You can change the path on your own, and, if you do, that could possibly change everything, good or not so good, in your life, depending upon which path you're on and which path you choose. There's no illusion to free will.

In the movie, *The Adjustment Bureau*,[3] one of the angels tells David Norris that, as humans, we do not have free will, just an illusion to make us think we actually have control of our own destiny. He says that if we had free will, it would be a disaster, and so The Bureau is around to make sure we don't make mistakes.

The question is, does God give us free will, or does He simply pull the strings and orchestrate everything around us? Is God the ultimate puppet master? Is He the master and are we his subjects? In the readings that I've been privileged to give to friends and co-workers, I remind them of one simple fact . . . God does indeed give us free will.

There's no certainty to life because life changes, evolves, breathes, and, with each breath, there's change, and, with each change, we also evolve and breathe.

The greatest gift anyone can have is freedom, and God gives that to us with unconditional love. Freedom to make mistakes and, at the same time, to make wondrous discoveries. Freedom to think inside the box or outside the box, or to create our own box. Freedom.

NAVIGATING THE MESSAGE—When I give readings, I always remind the person sitting across from me that free will can and probably will change some things in their life. It's the beauty of unconditional love. It's the beauty of free will.

CREATING SPACE FOR REFLECTION—We do not control free will and neither does the Universe. It's important to let go, so a person can make his or her own decisions and decide his or her own path.

MOVING FORWARD—Take a minute to sit back and just breathe because you know tomorrow things will change, and that's okay because you are indeed free. Enjoy that breath because you have the free will to do so.

The Awesomeness Paradigm

We live in a world of competition. It's basically all we do, if you think about it. We compete every minute of every day for people's attention, and when we don't get enough attention, we make damn sure that people notice us even more by telling everyone we meet and come in contact with how awesome we are and how blessed everyone is to have someone like us who is aglow with an aura of awesomeness, etc. You get the picture. We have to feel relevant.

Relevance is something we all struggle with in today's society.

I know I do, and I'm almost certain I'm not the only one. Today, because of social media like Facebook, Twitter, and Instagram, the need to be accepted is overwhelming.

We feel an obligation to tell everyone what we're doing at almost every point in our lives. Here's where we're going, here's what we're eating, here's what we're doing, here's what we're thinking, and here's what we're saying. I recall a friend of mine who years ago simply posted one word on Facebook: "Disney." I didn't know how to respond to the fact that he was among the thirty million or so who make the yearly pilgrimage to Orlando, the city where I reside, to go to Disney World, but by golly he got a ton of responses from everyone wishing they were there and, in some way, wishing they were him. Because, after all, he was displaying his awesomeness.

It's important to be accepted, or at least feel like we belong. After all, who doesn't want to belong? In the readings that I've been privileged to give to people, there's a hunger to be accepted. On the surface, the question, at first glance, appears to be, "Am I accepted?"

Below the surface, however, the question is actually, "Am I loved?" or more importantly, "Am I worthy of love?" The Universe accepts everyone and neglects no one. God is love and has bestowed upon us what Dr. Richard Rohr[4] calls "Original Blessing." We are covered in blessings–all love, all the time, everyone. It's an awesome feeling to be covered in the blessing blanket and not to be reminded constantly that we must cower under the cloak of sins all the time. Sure, we sin and fall short, but we're also loved unconditionally by God.

In church we sing, "Our God is an awesome God; He reigns from Heaven above with wisdom, power and love. Our God is an awesome God."[5] If we're made in the image of God and He is awesome, then aren't we awesome, too? Seems simple enough to me.

NAVIGATING THE MESSAGE—Being relevant in the world doesn't matter to the Universe, as you are an equal partner and therefore have been and will always be relevant and awesome at the same time.

CREATING SPACE FOR REFLECTION—You will always be important and will always be loved. If we believe we are made in the image and likeness of God, then everyone is deserving of love and deserving of all that the Universe has to offer. You give no one permission to tell you otherwise.

MOVING FORWARD—Next time you look in the mirror or catch a glimpse of yourself somewhere, learn to love that image of yourself. Say to yourself, "I am worthy. I am worthy. I am worthy." That person in the mirror has been waiting for someone to love them for a long time. That person is awesome.

Are Mystery Novels the Key to Our Future?

Everybody wants to know about the future. It's natural to want to know how things are going to turn out. In the readings I give to people, time and time again, the future comes up.

Relationships, finance, and health seem to be the three key priorities that everyone wants to know about. Will I fall in love? Will I get out of debt? Is my health okay? These are very innocent and well intentioned questions because let's face it, as humans we're naturally curious, and we want to know that there's light at the end of the tunnel.

The Universe doesn't work like that, and, quite honestly, I'm glad it doesn't.

Let me tell you about a reading that I gave to someone that involved the future. This person had unfortunately had a tough life, so as you can imagine, they wanted to know all about the future. During the reading, I could tell this person was getting restless because the Universe wasn't delivering what this person wanted. I kept telling the person over and over again, that's not the way it works.

This person wanted specific answers to specific questions, and all I could give was what the Universe was giving me. I could sense there was frustration building up, so I finally said to the person, "This isn't an exact science . . . nothing in life is always exact, perfect, and predictable." Some things came to fruition and some didn't. And I know for a fact that the things that did not happen in the timeline that I gave to this person did not sit well with them. I always caution people, as I did this person, that free will changes everything. I'm sure to this day they are still convinced that the Universe needs to spell out all the answers specifically and in great detail, leaving nothing to chance.

The Universe isn't a carnival game waiting to be played by people who want answers to every question under the sun. So what does all of this have to do with mystery novels?

Everyone loves a good mystery. The suspense and the waiting to see how everything ends, to see how the story unfolds and comes to a conclusion. How the characters end up and how the detective solves the mystery are what keep us turning the pages.

A good book, especially a mystery, is hard to put down once you're into it, once you commit yourself completely to the story. So, why is it that we become so fixated on the future?

Again, it's natural to want to know how our story will end, but it's the journey leading up to the end that keeps us spellbound and keeps us turning the pages. The conclusion or the end almost becomes secondary. It's like hearing the punchline before we hear the joke.

I've given readings in which I've told the person sitting across from me that, in three to six months, there will be a big change in their life, that this will be somewhat of a defining moment in their life. And I know that the person will focus on the destination three to six months from then and not the journey that it took to get there.

When giving readings that are psychic in nature, I always point out that the Universe will almost never tell us what to do because that circumvents God's free will.

God's unconditional love for us means we have unconditional free will.

To tell someone what is going to happen in the future is simply saying that, based on what the Universe sees at this time and based upon the path you are on, here's what is waiting for you on that path. The future is as uncertain as the present. But what is certain is the creator's love for us all. And we don't need to read a book to know that.

NAVIGATING THE MESSAGE—The challenge is that people become so fixated on a future in which something may or may not happen, that they completely forget everything (and everybody) on their current path. They don't enjoy the journey; they don't take the time to turn the pages and enjoy what the story is all about.

CREATING SPACE FOR REFLECTION—Do you simply shoot ahead to the ending and, in the process, miss a great story? Do you already know the ending of the story? Or do you wait with excitement and anticipation for how it will turn out? Remember that God is the author, but you're the editor.

MOVING FORWARD—Try living your life like a mystery novel. Enjoy each chapter, and, as long as you keep turning the pages, God will see to it that the end will be worth the wait.

The Wisdom of Hattori Hanzo

"Revenge is never a straight line. It's a forest, and like a forest, it's easy to lose your way . . . to get lost . . . to forget where you came in."

It never fails to inspire me that when I'm able to connect with people who have crossed over to the other side, they never mention or harbor any revenge or ill feelings for anyone. I've sat in many a mediumship circle when someone has come through that had harm done to them, or was abused in some way, and yet they are the ones asking for forgiveness and understanding for something they had done, not the other way around.

I've given readings in which someone is looking for answers to how their loved one died under what seemed to be mysterious circumstances. And the loved one comes through and simply gives a message of love, and says not to waste valuable time looking for answers that aren't going to change anything or which cause one to seek revenge or justice. Revenge is not important in the Universe.

Yes, you would think that the loved ones who have gone before us would give us the name or names of those who have done us wrong. But that's not on their mind or on their agenda. Their agenda is simply to help their loved ones here on the Earth plane move on with their lives and to tell us that they love us.

So, regarding the quote from the opening of this chapter—It's some of the last words spoken in the Quentin Tarantino movie *Kill Bill: Volume I*[6]—I know what you may be thinking, that this is an odd choice of a movie for a chapter on wisdom—but it does prove a major point.

The person who speaks these words is a character named Hattori Hanzo

. . . once the world's finest swordsman and maker of swords, who gave it up to live a life of peace. He agrees to give up that peace briefly to once again make the finest sword. Hanzo says of this sword, "If on your journey you should encounter God, God will be cut."

His words are a warning not only to the main character who is seeking revenge, but also a warning to us all. Now, the real Hattori Hanzo lived in the 1500s and is still, today, considered a major and respected figure in the history of Japan.

His bio is extremely impressive for not only his intelligence, strategy, and warrior spirit, but also for his willingness to seek God and live a life of peace.

When something bad happens to us, do we think that Karma will get the wrongdoer in the end? Contrary to popular belief, Karma is not revenge, Karma is enlightenment. It's a prayer that the person who does the bad deed will see the light of Karma and turn it around and do something good. Karma is a lesson learned, and when we seek revenge, there's no lesson to be learned.

NAVIGATING THE MESSAGE—Revenge is wasted effort and the Universe has no time for it. It serves no purpose in life and, at best, is only a fleeting moment of gratification that quickly wears away and ends up putting us on the level of the very same person who did us harm. And it never ever rights the wrong. Ever.

CREATING SPACE FOR REFLECTION—So, who have you wished revenge on lately? More importantly, who has wished revenge on us? For those who have not forgiven us, let's hope they find their way out of the forest.

MOVING FORWARD—It's time for you to turn around and go back to the light which shone upon us when we first entered the forest. Time to seek a new path for enlightenment. Time to move forward and leave the pain of revenge behind in the forest.

1. Pg. 37 - Delio, I. (2014). Quantum Entanglement. In: *CONSPIRE Conference*.
2. Pg. 39 - Fr. Richard Rohr-American, Franciscan Friar. Founder of the Center for Action and Contemplation.
3. Pg. 42 - *The Adjustment Bureau*. (2011). Directed by G. Nolfi. Universal Pictures.
4. Pg. 45 - Fr. Richard Rohr-American, Franciscan Friar. Founder of the Center for Action and Contemplation.
5. Pg. 45 - Mullins, R. (1988). Awesome God.
6. Pg. 49 - *Kill Bill Vol. 1*. (2003). Directed by Q. Tarantino. Miramax.

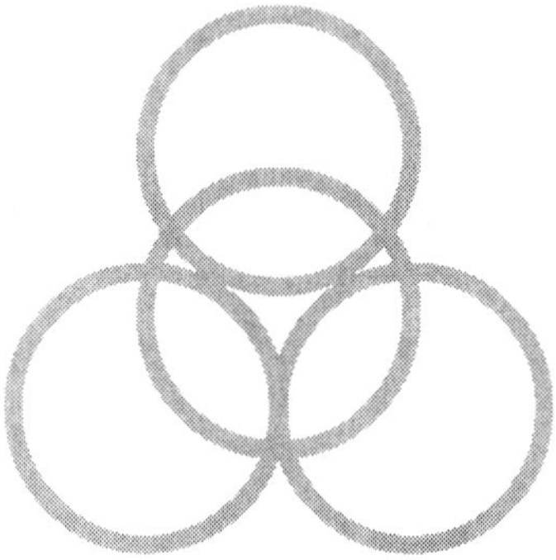

Chapter 4

SILENCE

Fingerprinting the Universe

During readings, I come across people who have feelings of self-doubt and low self-esteem. They feel they aren't worthy of love or anything else for that matter. They've been told most, if not all of their lives, that they simply do not matter. They've felt alone, abandoned, and hurt, and, to some extent, ashamed. I've sat across some folks that are in such a low place that they feel God doesn't love them and will never forgive them for what they've done in their lives. They feel isolated from the world.

The Universe never leaves its children. We are all connected, so no one is truly ever alone. If we're made in the image and likeness of our creator, then we are holy beings deserving of everything that this life has to offer. It is our heritage to have the imprint of the Divine bestowed upon us. We are a blessed people and that's the way the Universe wants us to look at it. We need to remember that we are loved unconditionally and are indeed worthy.

Edgar Cayce, one of the pioneers of the psychic/clairvoyant movement, had many tremendous moments in his career and made some insightful and thought-provoking statements along the way.

One of those statements is that we are "channels of divine energy." Cayce explains that this is the "universal message of mysticism and religion."[1]

So, if we can comprehend even a little bit of what Cayce is saying, then there's nothing we cannot do when it comes to the Universe.

There's nothing that is out of our reach, nothing that is out of bounds. Nothing is impossible when we have the imprint of the Divine within us. Our energy is the fingerprint of the Universe. Our soul never dies; instead, it provides oxygen for the Universe to grow and expand.

NAVIGATING THE MESSAGE—We are spiritual beings who happen to occupy a body. If we're made in the image of the creator, then we are truly holy beings who can transform time and space because we are channels of Divine energy.

CREATING SPACE FOR REFLECTION—The Universe is within us, and it's time we recognize that and embrace it. We do not need to look up, we need to look within.

MOVING FORWARD—Tonight, when your head hits the pillow, know that you are surrounded by love and light from the Universe. Know that you have worth and value to many, many people in this world. Know that you're an important person and everything you do touches, impacts, and influences everyone on this earth. And know that you do not have to reach for the stars, for they are already within you.

What Does Thinking of Nothing Look Like?

One of my greatest pleasures in life is just sitting around . . . doing nothing and thinking of nothing. Why does that give me hours and hours of pleasure?

One . . . because experts tell me that I'm wired that way as a man, and, two, again, according to experts, it makes me feel good.

Think about it . . . doing nothing sometimes makes us feel good.

In a society where we go, go, go, and are pushed to produce, produce, produce and win, win, win, doing nothing can be rewarding. Action-oriented people look at this as wasted time, when, in actuality, it is time well spent.

It makes absolutely no sense because society has trained us to be workaholics, in order to be successful.

Success . . . there's the holy grail of our very being and existence.

I could be wrong, but I don't recall seeing the word SUCCESS on many tombstones or grave markings in cemeteries. What does it matter how many times one was salesperson of the month or office manager of the year?

Mother Theresa of Calcutta said, "God does not require that we be successful, only that we be faithful."[2]

However, it is engrained in us at an early age that we have to be better than the next person . . . smarter . . . more attractive . . . more athletic . . . you get the picture.

Thinking of nothing can actually be *more* productive than thinking of everything, or at least a multitude of thoughts, projects, deadlines, etc. Why?

Because that's when the noise dies down. That's when the soul finally says, "Aaahhh . . . there you are," and can start to talk to you in a quiet voice.

Now, let me caution you on one thing, and this is a trap that I have fallen into: When we sit and attempt to think of nothing, there is a gap that we believe must be filled with thoughts.

As humans, we tend to think negatively about things, as it seems the human race is hell bent on being a race of self-fulfilling prophets.

When things don't always go our way, and we think the Universe is mustering all its resources to make our singular life miserable, we think negatively about everything and everybody, cursing the gods above with our fists clenched in the air, screaming about the injustices of the world. Please . . . get real.

I had a small plaque in my office for a number of years from the motivational product company, Successories,[3] that describes adversity as "A kite that flies higher against the wind than with it." Brilliant.

NAVIGATING THE MESSAGE—You cannot think of nothing all the time; but, every now and then it can cleanse the soul.

CREATING SPACE FOR REFLECTION—When the boundaries come down and you start to explore wondrous things in the universe just by thinking of nothing . . . now that is something to behold.

MOVING FORWARD—Great ideas are born out of exercises such as this, so sometime this week try it with zero expectations. Don't fill in the gap with negative thoughts, for they are not welcome. Time for your soul and you to get acquainted.

Lessons on Living from the Suicide Forest

I remember the day well. My youngest son was a sophomore in high school at the time. He came home one day and said he wanted to purchase a bass pedal from one of his closest friends at school. It was Christmastime and my wife and I agreed to purchase the bass pedal as one of his Christmas gifts. We gave him a check that was made out to his friend, Jay. Our son talked about what a great guy Jay was. They were part of a circle of friends that hung out before school and at lunchtime.

That day, however, isn't the day I remember well. It was the next day that I will never forget.

I was down in South Florida at a meeting, and at a break in the meeting I saw my son had called. I called him back and learned that Jay had taken his own life. Like that, he was gone.

Suicide had claimed yet another victim, and this time it was a sixteen-year-old boy. Unreal. My son was distraught and devastated, and so was the entire school.

Whether it's mental illness, depression, or a bad day, suicide rears its ugly head time and time again. I believe suicide touches us all, which makes the next story even more incredible.

Located in the northwest base of Mount Fuji lies Aokigahara, also known as the Suicide Forest. People come to this forest to be alone with their thoughts as they contemplate life.

They mainly contemplate whether or not to end their lives. Some come to end their lives quickly, and some come with their tents to be alone and think about whether or not life is worth living, about whether or not to carry on, and about whether or not anyone even cares if they live or die. The people who bring their tents have doubts about ending their lives.

People go there to be alone, but, in Aokigahara, no one is truly alone. They are among hundreds who have felt isolated and alone. It's ironic that in their final moments, they choose a place of silence and isolation to be among others who feel as they do. No one is ever truly alone. God is with us . . . the Universe is with us . . . Spirit is with us . . . Jesus and Mary Blessed Mother are with us . . . and our Spirit guides and teachers and angels from the highest realm are with us.

Japan has set up suicide patrols to go in and locate the tents where there is a glimmer of hope that dwells inside. These patrols mainly just talk to the people and get them to think and see their life in a different light. We all have people in our lives who help us see things in a different light. Are there "sign patrols" in your life that help you shed light on the good and wondrous things that you encounter every day?

We are never, ever truly alone.

And remember, you also serve a purpose in helping others to see their path more clearly. We're all in this together.

NAVIGATING THE MESSAGE—Everyone needs a comforting word . . . everyone needs someone to talk to . . . everyone needs someone to come along and just listen. Could this somebody be you?

CREATING SPACE FOR REFLECTION—We're not so different from those who enter the forest. The question is, what have we learned from them?

MOVING FORWARD—Take a few minutes today and quiet yourself with your eyes wide open. Relax. All will be well with you, for you are a child of the Universe.

Does Our Conversation with the Universe Get Lost in Translation?

Being clairvoyant presents its own set of challenges, mainly because it's not always clear what language the Universe is using at the time. Here's what I mean . . . I see images and pictures that are either symbolic or literal. The only way for me to know what I'm seeing is to slow down the images, so I can decipher the language the Universe is using. And the only way for me to decipher is to ask questions and listen.

Symbols mean different things to different people; but, it's important to remember that the Universe is showing these images to me for a reason, and that reason may only be known to the person or persons sitting across from me. The only way for me to pass along the images and pictures that are passing before me is to be silent and listen.

When we talk or attempt to talk to the Universe, what language do we use?

Do we ever consider using the language of the Divine? More importantly, what is the language of the Divine? We often associate language with the spoken word, but have we ever thought of silence as a language? In order to have a conversation with God, we have to consider using silence as the language of the Divine.

We seem to think that in order to talk to God we have to do all the talking. A conversation is a two-way street, meaning, at some point, we have to be quiet and listen. In today's world, so many noises, voices, and sounds drown out what the Divine is attempting to tell us, show us, and help us experience.

How many times do we have conversations in our daily lives with people in which points and parts of the conversation get lost in the translation? Why is that? We talk over each other, interrupt each other, and sometimes we even turn off the other person midway through the conversation because we're constructing our response to what they are saying. So, we don't truly hear what the other person is saying.

Having a conversation means you have to participate. To participate, we have to engage in proactive listening. Think about it . . . the creator wants to talk to us, and we're too busy to listen, or we already know it all, so, therefore, have no need to listen.

It's time we learn the language of the Divine by listening and learning not to respond, but to digest, reflect, and hopefully to put into practice what we have learned in the conversation. When we do that, then it's a win-win for us, and for the Universe. And isn't that what good, productive conversations are meant to do?

NAVIGATING THE MESSAGE—To learn a language and even participate in a language that is familiar to us, we have to proactively and passionately listen. It's how we learn. How many times have you heard someone speak in a different language than yours and said to yourself, "That's a beautiful language?" If we want to learn, we have to slow down, listen very carefully, and hang on every word.

CREATING SPACE FOR REFLECTION—Try this: sit in silence for five minutes a day. It's downright difficult at times, but eventually you may learn to tolerate it, or even like it. Maybe you'll even look forward to it.

Think about it . . . silence has no expectations other than to show up.

The Universe will then see this as a regularly scheduled appointment, so to speak, and start to talk to you.

MOVING FORWARD—Sitting in silence may not be your thing; you can also try going outside in nature and taking it all in or go for a quiet walk. Unlike sitting forever in a doctor's office, the Universe will not keep you waiting. However, in order to have a real conversation, you have to show up and be engaged. A conversation is for participants. Time for you to participate. After all, the appointment has already begun.

Blinded by Silence

Silence has always been a big part of my readings. When the Universe speaks or shows me words, images, or pictures, or loved ones who have transitioned over to the Spirit world, it can be challenging to comprehend what I'm seeing, hearing, and experiencing.

This is mainly because the messages are appearing at a high rate of speed. The Spirit world operates at a much higher level and dimension, and at a higher and faster frequency within the Universe than we do here on the Earth plane.

This is where silence comes in. At the beginning of the reading, I always inform the person in front of me that there will be periods of silence in which I'm attempting to slow down the speed of messages and images by asking questions.

This is so I can interpret signs, images, pictures, etc. for the person who is receiving the reading, and periods of silence are sometimes necessary for this to happen.

I'm reminded of a particular reading that I gave a young lady once. She was genuinely open to the messages that the Universe was giving her, but she seemed extremely impatient, wanting to know everything right then and there, and in painstaking detail. Only by slowing everything down and spending a couple of minutes in silence interpreting the signs, did the messages really come alive for her and start to make sense. This was also the message that the Universe was giving her . . . to slow down and spend some time in silence. I recommended to her, as I do virtually everyone, to spend some time in silence, for only then can answers to questions be revealed.

The Mothership has one big ASK for you to consider.

Alone- Spend some time alone. This doesn't mean you're lonely, it simply means alone. Some of the greatest and wisest teachers and philosophers in the world needed time alone to gather their thoughts and block out the distractions of daily life.

Silence- Spend time in silence. Just sit in silence . . . that's it. No expectations but to listen and be. So much noise goes on every minute of our lives that finding some time to be quiet is virtually impossible. But when we do, it is Heaven on earth. Some of the greatest thinkers and minds in the world set aside for themselves a considerable amount of quiet time.

Know- Be confident and know that the steps that you are taking to get closer to the Universe will be worth it. The closer we get, the more knowledge that will be imparted to us.

NAVIGATING THE MESSAGE—To truly escape and start to learn to channel, we have to learn to not *escape* from ourselves.

Being quiet is something we struggle with because we cannot seem to find the time to escape the noise. Spending time alone is something we struggle with because being alone means that we are separated from others, and, to some of us, that is a scary proposition.

CREATING SPACE FOR REFLECTION—We come to terms with who we are so that the Universe can converse with us, without interruptions, commercials, or noise. Pause today and see if that one little interruption in your busy and hectic schedule doesn't make a difference.

MOVING FORWARD—What does being quiet sound like? What does being alone feel like? Try it a couple of times and see what happens.

Go on a solitary walk in nature and see how the trees, the earth, the wind, the sounds all around you embrace your every move. That's the language of the Universe, and you will want to dial it up again.

Answering the Cosmic Phone

I fondly remember the days of placing collect calls to ensure that the other party paid for it, or at least you hoped they picked up and told the operator, "I accept." I remember reversing the charges a couple of times, and I also remember those times when I waited until after a certain time in the evening or a certain day of the week to place a long distance call because the rates were lower.

I believe most of those days are gone, as we have moved on with new technology and new ways to connect with one another. The Universe, however, hasn't moved on. It's here among us still waiting for some of us to call. Remember those times when we would call just to check up on someone, to see how they're doing? The Universe wants us to do the same; because in order to have a conversation, both parties have to talk and listen.

I know what you're thinking, and it's something that I also thought for a long time. "I've been here all this time, and the Universe hasn't talked to me." Except the Universe *has* been talking to us all of our lives, and we just haven't paid attention. We've paid attention to other things but not to the Universe. I'm sure there have been times when you've thought of something, dismissed it, and then someone mentions exactly what you were thinking. That's one of the many ways the Universe speaks to us.

You will be thinking of someone who had passed, and suddenly you see something, feel something, or hear a song that brings that person closer to you. You see a set of numbers that appear out of nowhere and it's the date or anniversary of someone's birthday or passing. The Universe has many ways to connect.

I remember fighting the urge to meditate because it was boring and nothing seemed to happen. To me, it seemed like a huge waste of time. I would sit there and just wait for the time to end. A voice inside kept saying, "Keep at it, Jerry, and if nothing else, learn patience." And I did. And it has paid off. Now, after years of resisting the voice that kept telling me to meditate, I look forward to spending those times getting to know my creator better by sitting in the midst of the Universe.

The patience I learned was key for me to develop my gifts. I thought since I learned about these gifts later in life, I was behind and had to make up for lost time.

After all, it seemed that every other medium and psychic that I ran across or read about had these gifts early in life, and that frustrated me. I couldn't understand why I was chosen to bring forth and develop these gifts later in life, until I discovered that the Universe had been talking to me for years, and I just didn't pick up the "cosmic phone" to speak or return the call.

I discovered that it was my time in this life to step forward and help people and that the Universe would clear the paths for me to do so. To this day, the path has become clearer and clearer, and yours will, too.

NAVIGATING THE MESSAGE—The cosmic phone has many lines and many ways to connect. Like the Universe, it is vast and never ending, and there is no need for someone to call between the hours of 9:00 p.m. and 1:00 a.m. to fix the lines. The lines are never broken, never down, and there's never a weak connection.

CREATING SPACE FOR REFLECTION—What paths do you need cleared in your life to make room for the Divine? How can we clear the path and the boundaries in our lives so that there is room?

MOVING FORWARD—There is one thing that you must do. I'm sure you remember the times that your mom or dad told you to turn down the TV because they couldn't hear the person on the other end of the phone, right? It's the same with using the cosmic phone.

Turn off the TV, turn off the cell phone, and pick a place that's nice and quiet. Even if it's only for a few minutes. Trust me . . . you're going to want to hear what the Universe has to say.

The Art of Contemplating Intuition

What kind of chapter title is this for a book about psychic and medium gifts?

Does this have anything whatsoever to do with messages from the Universe?

Yes, it has everything to do with messages from the Universe. Here's why: Our intuition is our soul talking to us, and our soul is oxygen for the Universe. They are linked together forever, so when we hear a voice inside our head telling us to do something, it would be worthwhile to sit for a few minutes and contemplate what that voice is telling us. What if that voice is our intuition attempting to tell us something? Seems like a worthy cause to me.

So, what are those voices in our head? And what do they want? Why are they constantly after us? It is intuition . . . intuition is speaking to us. So, if that's the case, then why don't we listen?

The voices in our head are drowned out by noise that we hear every day. There's no escaping the sounds that seem to engulf us no matter where we go in life. There is no silence for us to enjoy. There isn't any sanctuary for our intuition to seek shelter. So, what is intuition saying? Listen and learn.

NAVIGATING THE MESSAGE—What is it about intuition that we choose not to hear . . . not to participate . . . not to listen? It is the Universe speaking to us, and the only way for us to comprehend it is to contemplate intuition.

CREATING SPACE FOR REFLECTION—Look back at each day and consider if you felt or heard something that seemed out of place in your mind, your thoughts, and your day. Voices that you didn't pay attention to. The random thoughts (clean, of course) that appeared out of nowhere–where did they come from? What did they mean? Contemplating their meaning is going to take some effort, but your intuition is worth it. My life has changed dramatically since I started to listen to my inner voice, as I call my intuition. Your life will change, too.

Time and time again I tell people during readings to listen to their intuition, as it is the Universe talking to them.

MOVING FORWARD—Stay tuned for more thoughts, for they will certainly come your way. Embrace these thoughts and the voice that your soul is using to talk to you. Pay attention; keep your mindset on and don't turn the channel.

---

1. Pg. 54 - Reed, H. (1989). *Edgar Cayce on Channeling Your Higher Self.* Grand Central Publishing, p.14.
2. Pg. 55 - Mother Theresa of Calcutta, Catholic Nun and Saint.
3. Pg. 56 - Successories.com. (2017). *Successories Motivational Posters, Employee Recognition Gifts & Awards.* [online]

Chapter 5

DISCOVERY

Say Hello to Your Better Half

I must disclaim that this section is from one man's point of view. I apologize for this in advance. So, I have a man crush on Fr. Richard Rohr[1], a Franciscan priest who is so eloquent that I'm convinced God talks straight through him. I'm so envious, but, at the same time, grateful that someone like this exists, and that I've met him and talked with him, and even got to help facilitate a retreat with him.

According to Fr. Richard Rohr, your false self is the self that others might view you as, especially amongst men in the business world. It's not negative, it's not bad, this false self of yours . . . it's just simply not your true self. Think of your true self as your better half. Your false self is not a bad half, it's just not truly who you are as a person.

Society tends to value men in one main vein: our job, our work, and our career. Society constantly reminds us that a man's worth–or, in other words, man's value to society–is defined by his livelihood.

It's why so many men in their 30s, 40s, and especially their 50s and beyond, seem to lose their identity when they lose their livelihood, either by their choice or their company's choice. Society has inadvertently told us men . . . without your job, what use are you?

I worked for a great company as a salesman, but that wasn't my true self. That was just one part of who I am. However, it doesn't tell the whole story of who I am, and there's the false self.

I am a sales person, an account manager, a father, a grandfather, a son, a brother, an uncle, a father-in-law, a husband, a friend, a son-in-law, an author, a psychic, a medium, a clairvoyant, an associate, a lover of the Universe, a Catholic, a Spiritualist, a student, a fan of Notre Dame, etc. I am many things, and so are you.

My better half was awakened in 2010 when I discovered gifts from God of psychic mediumship and clairvoyance. The second half of life is in essence our better half of life. Therefore, we are our better half. It is time for you to say hello to your better half and use your gifts. Our better half is inside us waiting like a clock, and the louder the clock ticks, the more our soul will tell us to turn off the alarm and get moving.

NAVIGATING THE MESSAGE—We are sons and daughters of the Universe, loved unconditionally by God, embraced by Spirit, and urged to do great things on this planet.

CREATING SPACE FOR REFLECTION—Never let anyone tell you differently. You do not give your company, your job, or your career permission to define you as a person. You also do not give them permission to hurt you. A wise Franciscan priest[2] once told me that he loved being a priest, but he never gave the Catholic Church permission to hurt him.

MOVING FORWARD—Only you have the right to define yourself as a person, and you will never give it up. You own you. No one else does. Say hello to your better half.

Approaching the Wall of Shame

In the readings that I've been privileged to give, I often encounter walls, Walls that people have put up for years to protect them from whatever it is that all of us keep buried deep within our souls. Our souls are hidden from everybody and everything except for the Universe, and that's because the soul is part of the Universe. The Universe knows all and is willing to help with all, but the wall of shame often gets in the way.

Whatever it is that we feel ashamed of builds upon our soul brick by painful brick until it is a wall that we cannot begin to climb over, around, or through.

Walls. They keep us in, they protect us, they give us comfort, they define boundaries, and they keep our enemies out.

They also blind us to the world outside. They block us. They give false impressions of the world, and they keep our friends and sometimes our faith out. They also make it difficult to listen to the Divine.

But they do keep us comfortable—too comfortable.

We encounter walls in our lives—in fact, multiple times throughout the day.

Unfortunately, some walls that we encounter in our lives define us. So, why is that? Shame is one of those key walls that surrounds and engulfs us.

When we break down walls or attempt to go beyond them, we somehow feel exposed, vulnerable, weak . . . in other words, not worthy. We simplyx don't approach the wall because we feel it's not worth it. We need to remember that we get out of life what we put in.

NAVIGATING THE MESSAGE—It's time to shed that skin of guilt, time to move on, and time to go down the path of enlightenment. It will be worth the effort.

CREATING SPACE FOR REFLECTION—Guilt, for whatever reason, should never define who we are as a person or as a people. We are made in the eyes of the creator. We have God's unconditional love. There's no shame in that, and there's also no strings attached.

MOVING FORWARD—It's time to cut the strings that we do believe are attached and approach the walls that we have built within our souls. And there's no better wall to approach than shame? Whatever it is that you feel ashamed of, don't you think it's high time you approach that wall to see what's on the other side?

The question is, what will you find beyond the wall of shame? In the end, it's only a wall.

Hanging on to the Thought of Letting Go

At the beginning of every reading that I give, I say a prayer of protection to the Universe that nothing negative can enter into the reading. I ask for my Spirit Guides from the Universe, from the Spirit world, and the Spirit Guides of the person sitting across from me to send me any messages to pass along that will help the person. Spirit Guides are people who have passed on and are in the Spirit world. They have been around to help us our entire lives, even though we may not have known they were there. They are here to help us through the trials and tribulations of our lives and get us past the negative fences that keep us from reaching our full potential.

Sometimes those fences are meant to keep us in, at least long enough to examine a little bit about our baggage that we hold onto.

I have done readings for numerous friends and clients who, for one reason or another, had held onto particular things in their lives for a long, long time. Those negative fences wouldn't let them examine their own baggage, much less get out and get on with their lives.

Letting go . . . we talk about it almost non-stop. "I just need to let go," or "Time to let go."

How many times do we get rid of our baggage or look to the heavens and say, "God, this time, I'm really letting go," only to have the same baggage in our lives again? Why does that baggage stay with us? Have we examined everything about the baggage?

It's like New Year's resolutions repeated over and over again and broken over and over again. Why? We're never prepared to let go because, all of our lives, society has told us that we need to hold on to things, then tells us that we need to let go of those same things.

The question is . . . why? Why do we need to let go of people? Places? Things? Feelings? Ideas? Emotions? Relationships? Again, the question is, why?

NAVIGATING THE MESSAGE—Why not hold on to ideas, feelings, emotions . . . all those things listed above, at least long enough to see what it is about those things that we feel we need to let go of?

Why not examine what we feel we need to let go of a little bit closer, to see what it is that makes us uncomfortable?

CREATING SPACE FOR REFLECTION—When I give readings, there is so much that the Universe tries to convey to the person across from me, especially when it comes to learning from the past. It makes sense sometimes not to let go of things until we learn what those things meant to us. Spirit Guides from the Universe are there to help us.

MOVING FORWARD—Next time, if there's something that you think you need to let go of, pause and ask that something, "What is it about you that makes me want to get rid of you?" The answer just might surprise you.

The Hidden Message Behind *A Charlie Brown Christmas*

We all have security blankets that we hold on to, sometimes forever, for fear of letting go and experiencing failure. We've all experienced setbacks and challenges in our lives, and sometimes we feel like we just can't face one more.

There have been countless times when I have offered a reading to a friend after I have found out they were interested, only for them to back out, saying how afraid they were. They simply didn't want to know anything that was going to happen in their life that might be negative. Their security blanket was not knowing anything about the past, the present, or the future. Their security blanket was simply a concern built around the fact that I might find out something about them. Their security blanket was not wanting to be judged because, if they dropped their blanket, it might expose a weakness for all of the world to see.

This is the furthest thing from my mind. The Universe is there to help people, not hurt them.

I believe most of us have seen the beloved holiday classic *A Charlie Brown Christmas*.[3] This simple little cartoon didn't use professional child voice actors, and yet was an instant classic, as half of the TV sets in America tuned in that night.

When you read the background story of how this classic came to be–and almost wasn't made–there, for me, was this hidden message.

The hidden message is contained in what is arguably the most magical two minutes in TV . . . when Linus explains the true meaning of

Christmas and quotes from Luke's Gospel.

It's also one of the few times you will ever see Linus let go of his beloved security blanket.

"Fear not for behold . . . I bring you great tidings of Joy."

Linus lets go of his fear and his security blanket for a good cause and a good reason.

It's this letting go of the blanket that gets to me, and, yes . . . according to the creators of *Peanuts*,[4] it was done on purpose.

I'm about to embark on yet another aspect of my clairvoyant, medium, psychic journey, and, yes, I've been holding onto my security blanket for far too long, so now it's time to let go and behold God's wondrous tidings of joy. What about you?

NAVIGATING THE MESSAGE—The security blankets we all hold on to need to be dropped at some point in life.

CREATING SPACE FOR REFLECTION—Are you ready to trust in the Universe and drop your security blanket, if only for a moment?

MOVING FORWARD—Embrace your fears and let go of your security blanket. The Universe is calling you to do so. The Mothership wants you to be courageous.

If Linus can do it . . . so can you. Peace.

Take Five and Get Comfortable with the Uncomfortable

I worked as part of a training team for over a decade, training numerous people in various positions in sales and retail. Everything from teaching store associates how to greet customers when they come into the store, to training company associates how to do an expense report.

The training director was a great guy who taught me many things, and one of the things he said repeatedly was, "Get comfortable with the uncomfortable." That was a lesson of sorts to try new things, to have new experiences, to go beyond conventional wisdom, and to push the boundaries. Take chances and a leap of faith with life. Such was the case of Paul Desmond.

In 1959, Paul Desmond, as part of the Dave Brubeck Quartet, wrote the groundbreaking jazz piece, "Take Five,"[5] which was written in 5/4 time instead of the usual 4/4 time of most jazz pieces. It certainly didn't fit into any conventional music that was playing at the time. Critics hated it.

Critics said that it was clumsy and awkward, and that people wouldn't listen to it, much less dance to it. Yet much to their surprise, young people filled the dance floors of ballrooms from coast to coast dancing the night away to what would become the biggest selling jazz single of all time. It's one of the reasons that I love jazz music, as it pushes the boundaries and borders and becomes almost free-flowing. Jazz music reminds me of a night at the Improv, where anything goes. The Universe reminds me of jazz music.

It took me some time to get used to having people who had passed talk to me, appear before me, and teach me lessons about life.

It took some time for me to get used to hearing voices from the Universe. It took some time for me to get used to giving messages and readings and being as skeptical as one can be.

I was very uncomfortable doing all of this, but yet, somehow, I persevered, and you will, too.

In order to disconnect from the noise of the world and connect to the Universe, we need to take some time to reflect upon the day's events, either before we go to bed or when we wake up.

By listening to the day, we just might learn what God, the Universe, and Spirit is attempting to teach, ask, or tell us. It will be uncomfortable and fantastic at the same time.

NAVIGATING THE MESSAGE—We cannot have a conversation with the Mothership unless we find a few minutes each day to charge our "soul batteries". Our temple of Divine energy needs to be recharged to help us deal with the noise of the day and to teach us, if nothing else, patience. With patience, we learn to deal with things in life that make us uncomfortable.

CREATING SPACE FOR REFLECTION—Consider reflecting on those things that make you uncomfortable in life. What makes you squirm, but, more importantly, *why* does it make you squirm ?

Take a few minutes to reach deep down within you to see what it is you need to address with the uneasiness that you feel. Just five minutes a day to converse with the Higher Side of Life about these concerns is all the Universe is asking. We will call it a "High Five."

MOVING FORWARD—It's time you get comfortable with the uncomfortable. Your arms and legs aren't going to fall off. The world is not going to end. Examine what it is that makes you uncomfortable. Time to "Take Five." See you on the dance floor.

The Fear of Being Afraid

I gave a reading one time to a lady whose energy was so strong that it was actually overwhelming. There were some things that she really wanted in life, and she wanted them to happen and to be true so bad that the vibrations were extremely high. The messages that I received and subsequently gave to her ended up on a positive note, and she was extremely pleased with the results. Weeks later, however, the messages ended up on a not-so-positive note. They were the complete opposite from what I gave her a few weeks earlier.

So, what's so fearful about that? I was afraid that I had messed up. That I gave this nice lady an incorrect reading. That I had led her astray. That I had failed. In actuality, it was her energy which had overwhelmed and affected the reading. These things can happen; but I had fear of failing as a psychic medium. Fear is one of the emotions that can be an enemy and an ally at the same time.

Fear . . . one of the greatest motivators we have in life . . . fear, at any time of the year, is widespread and doesn't feel like a great motivator at times.

Fear of holiday cheer, fear of not being in the right place at the right time, fear of depression, fear of not having friends around, fear of not having family around, fear of our neighbors not being like we are, fear of someone not acting like we think they should act, fear of being alone, we will insert something we're afraid of . . .

But fear is a great motivator, as well, because it is fear that drives men and women to accomplish their greatest achievements. Fear can push us towards greatness.

However, it is fear that causes us not to open the gifts that God, Spirit, and the Universe have given us. Fear of the unknown and what will be expected of us when we do open the gift(s) from the Universe. Time to get over it folks; open the gifts.

When someone gives you a gift, it is meant to be opened, unwrapped, and shared.

NAVIGATING THE MESSAGE—Forget the New Year's resolutions that you know within thirty days will be a thing of the past. Begin now and contemplate, meditate, and reflect upon the gifts that everyone around you has said God and Spirit have given you.

CREATING SPACE FOR REFLECTION—Time to awaken from the slumber and realize your potential as a child of God. God chose these gifts for you when you came into this world, so don't be afraid. Spirit provided the paper, and the Universe wrapped it. Ponder these gifts and embrace the fears.

MOVING FORWARD—It's up to you. Let the fear of not knowing drive you to open the gifts of destiny that God has chosen for you.

Guilt Is Like Crossing a River . . . Easier to Navigate Once You Understand the Depth

You don't have to be Catholic to feel guilty about things. Trust me, I know, as I have inside me burdens of guilt that I have carried all of my life. It's either a badge of shame or a backpack that weighs us down, but weigh us down it does. We have regrets and things that we wished we had never done, and it's like a wall that we cannot break through or get around.

When I connect to Spirit and people who have crossed over come forward to speak or deliver a message to a loved one who is sitting across from me, you can bet that there's going to be some mention of guilt that the person in front of me, for whatever reason, is holding on to. And that the one who has passed is telling that loved one to move on with their life, and that all is forgiven.

Sometimes the one who has passed is asking for forgiveness in order to move on in the Spirit world. Forgiveness is a double-edged sword, and sometimes the edges are so sharp that both parties get cut.

Spirit seems to understand this in an incredible way.

During readings that I've given, guilt is one thing that rears its ugly head time and time again. People who sit across from me or who are on the other end of the phone try to hide the ways in which they have led their lives with the shadow of guilt following them everywhere they go. On the surface, and perhaps buried deep within us, are things we regret. We've all been there, and in all likelihood will be there again. Guilt seems to be the one thing that binds us, that keeps us all connected. Mainly because we all feel like we can never be forgiven for "sins of the past."

It is difficult to move on when we feel this way. It is difficult to fulfill our purpose in life when there are chains that need to be unshackled because of decisions that were made in the past. Decisions still seem to haunt us. The very depth of our guilt lies within our soul, and therein lies the knowledge to fully understand what it is that keeps us from moving forward. It all starts with that first step.

NAVIGATING THE MESSAGE—It's a little more manageable to get through your daily routine when you forgive yourself and acknowledge that, every now and then, we fall short of perfection. We fall short of being generous, or nice, or spiritual, or loving. We just fall short. Period.

CREATING SPACE FOR REFLECTION—Face it, we make mistakes, sometimes some very big mistakes; and we hurt people, sometimes in a big way. Even if you're not Christian, let us consider one thing that Jesus said and did. He tried to take away our guilt, so that we could progress forward and live life to its fullest. Guilt will absolutely eat you alive if you allow it. What's done is done. It's as simple as that.

MOVING FORWARD—Time to cross the river and shed the shroud of guilt that you wear. Guilt never looks good on anyone, and it is never in season. Get in the water and don't worry about the depth; like guilt, it just looks deeper than it really is.

---

1. Pg. 71 - Fr. Richard Rohr-American, Franciscan Friar. Founder of the Center for Action and Contemplation.
2. Pg.72 - Franciscan-Religious Order within Catholic Church, St Francis.
3. Pg. 78 - *A Charlie Brown Christmas.* (1965). Directed by B. Melendez and C. Schultz. Lee Mendelson Films.
4. Pg. 79 - Schultz, C. (1950-2000). *Peanuts.*
5. Pg. 80 - Desmond, P. (1959). Take Five. Columbia Records.

Chapter 6

HOPE

As Long as There's a Pulse, There's a Heartbeat

How does one move on from a personal tragedy?

During readings, it is obvious that some folks just cannot move on and still are tied down by the tragedies and setbacks in their lives. That's understandable for all of us. It's tough to let go of the past and move on; but time and time again, during readings, the one thing that the Universe says repeatedly is keep moving, keep moving, and, most of all, keep moving.

Don't be planted so deep in the past that you cannot grow in the future. I remember one particular reading that I gave to a very sharp and impressive young lady. I could tell there was something troubling her, and, sure enough, the Universe dug it out so she could address it. She was so sure that I was going to judge her, and that God would never forgive her, that it was holding her back. I told her that no one is going to judge her, and that the Universe loves her unconditionally and wants her to move on with her life. The relief that she showed was amazing, and it was obvious that the burden had been lifted. Her heartbeat to her path in life was thumping again.

How do we cope with tragedies and allow ourselves to move on?

I've lived in Orlando for over thirty years, and I could have never imagined the horror that fell on June 12, 2016, at the Pulse nightclub. Orlando had never experienced anything like it, as a gunman opened fire and killed forty-nine innocent people and injured another fifty-three. It was a senseless tragedy and senseless loss of life. Innocent people were just dancing and having a good time. Pulse was not just a gay nightclub as the media reported; it was a place where gay and straight came to have a good time and dance the night away. It was seen by many as a safe place to go and enjoy life.

A young lady in my neighborhood lost four of her closest friends that night. Think about it, sometimes it takes a lifetime to lose four friends, and she lost them in one night.

One of the most amazing things that I and others witnessed was the immediate long lines to donate blood . . . some three hours long. Blood. The very thing that we all need to survive, to keep our hearts pumping and to keep our PULSE alive.

Blood for straight and gay alike, from friends and strangers, from Hispanic or not, from male or female, from young or old . . . blood to give life and hope to the hopeless. This is how you move on from a tragedy. This city united like never before, all around a common goal: the respect for life and for our fellow human beings. As Marilyn Awtry[1] says, "We are Spirit with a body, not the other way around." If we believe that, then the body almost becomes irrelevant in the grand scheme of things. We are Spirit, plain and simple.

NAVIGATING THE MESSAGE—Being gay, or straight, or lesbian, or whatever labels society puts on us all seems less and less important when people rally around a common cause.

What does seem important is what the Universe tells us every day: love is the answer.

Jesus said to "love your neighbor as yourself," so it's high time we start.

CREATING SPACE FOR REFLECTION—Take a moment to remember those who lost their lives to either senseless brutality or tragedy. Carry their hopes and dreams within our hearts, the very same organ that gives us our PULSE.

MOVING FORWARD—It's time to unshackle those chains that have bound you with whatever tragedies have befallen you, and move on with your life. As the forty-nine victims from the PULSE massacre know, life is too short to waste.

The Ultimate Endgame

Early in the development of my gifts, I struggled with a number of things, among them religion and Catholicism. I'm Catholic, and the Catholic Church doesn't endorse my gifts. The Church looks upon the gifts of mediumship, psychic, and clairvoyance as something other than spiritual. Time after time, I would hear or see references to the Bible that indicated these gifts came from someone or something other than God.

This bothered me considerably and was always in the back of my mind. Was I doing something wrong, or were these gifts of a dark or negative nature? So, when is a gift a gift? How do we discern God's gifts to us? How do we know if it's a gift at all? I recently posed this question to a Franciscan priest whom I hold in high regard.

I asked him about the "gifts" of psychic, mediumship and clairvoyance, and his answer was simple: "Jerry, it is faith, hope, charity; that's the litmus test for any gift that we are seeking answers for." Faith, hope, charity, the three theological virtues that allow man/woman to share in God's nature. The answer that I had been seeking. Here's how I interpreted his answer:

Faith- Does the gift deepen your faith in God?

Hope- Does the gift give hope to others? Do you help the downtrodden? Does it give hope to the hopeless?

Charity- Does the gift become an act of charity to others? Are you charitable to others through the gift?

I put a check mark beside all of the above, and I found the validation

I had been seeking. The gifts that I do believe we're all given do come from and through God in order for us to grow and help others. That's the ultimate endgame.

NAVIGATING THE MESSAGE—Another close friend of mine once asked me, "Jerry, in what you do, does it draw you closer to God?" He went on to say that God doesn't care what you do, as long as it draws you closer to Him. It draws you closer to Spirit, and, in the end, draws you closer to the Universe. The question is, does it draw me closer to all of the above?

CREATING SPACE FOR REFLECTION—Take some time tonight to think about tomorrow to see if there are a couple of things you can do just to draw yourself a little bit closer to God. It could be giving thanks for your health or your friends, etc. It could be saying a quiet little prayer, even to yourself, before you sit down to eat. It's all good and it all works.

MOVING FORWARD—Are your actions drawing you closer to the Divine? Look at your daily routine. If what you do on a daily basis draws you closer to God, then you're on the right path. If not, then it's time for a litmus test.

Baseball and the Mothership

The curve ball is considered one of the toughest pitches to hit, for new major leaguers and players of all ages. It is something to behold when it's thrown correctly.

Why? Because it starts out as one thing and ends up as something else.

Our lives are like that . . . our lives start out as something that we imagine, visualize, and dream, and it ends up being entirely something else. Life changes, and we change along with it.

Something that no one could see or imagine comes our way, and it scares the hell out of us, mainly because we never saw it coming. We didn't plan or prepare for it. Tragedy, sorrow, death, racism, denial, bankruptcy, disappointment . . . the list is endless.

Our gifts from God are like that; our lives are going perfectly fine, and then it happens . . . God asks us to do something that we, in a million years, would never consider, never dream of, never think about doing or even attempting to do.

My gifts of psychic, mediumship, and clairvoyance rose to the surface and made themselves known to me, all at the tender young age of fifty-five, and I never saw it coming. People who had known me all of my life were stunned to find that I was now a "fortune teller." They were shocked–and probably a little dismissal of the fact–that I was now touting these gifts as a way of helping people.

And who could blame them? I was thrown a curveball and simply couldn't begin to comprehend it either.

The Universe is all about throwing curve balls at us in what Carl Jung[2] and others call "the second half of life." In the first half of life, we lay down foundations; we plant seeds; we build, provide, and construct–all fast-ball pitches.

In the second half of life, we're called to learn how to hit the curve ball in the way of thinking, contemplating, and leaving a legacy behind. What will your legacy be?

NAVIGATING THE MESSAGE—We are called to learn new and wondrous things, to teach and learn from others, and to be non-judgmental.

CREATING SPACE FOR REFLECTION—Issues and things we set aside or pushed away in the first half of life now call to us to embrace them and learn.

MOVING FORWARD—People that we have judged, criticized, and even despised . . . it's now time to learn from them.

The only way for us to evolve, grow, and advance is to learn. Here comes the windup and the pitch.

John Mayer Was So Close

John Mayer sang, "Your Body Is a Wonderland,"[3] and I believe he was on to something. I look at people who practice yoga, and I'm convinced that the human body is more than just a wonderland. I'm in awe of the human body and how it responds to the Universe. Folks who engage in yoga are doing much, much more than exercise. They are connecting with the Universe in a spiritual and metaphysical way by expressing their bodies in a meditative state. Your body is a source of light and energy, so it doesn't seem farfetched that you can actually harness and channel energy.

Everything in this world moves with energy and vibrations. Your body and everything around your body moves and never stops moving. Like the Universe, it's always moving and breathing and, at the same time, connecting to everything that is moving and breathing.

That, my friends, is channeling. So, let's look at channeling in another way.

According to the legendary psychic/clairvoyant, Edgar Cayce,[4] your body is a Channel that can pick up energy and vibrations.

In fact, Cayce goes one step further and says your body is a channel of "divine energy." Now does the example of yoga make sense? We have heard for years that the body is a temple; so, if this is true, then think of your body as a temple of Divine energy. This temple allows us to have a conversation with the Universe. The temple is sacred, and so is the Universe.

Everything in this world and the next is powered by energy and vibrations. Everything moves and everything is alive whether we choose to believe it or not.

NAVIGATING THE MESSAGE—Edgar Cayce[5] was one of the very first to use the word/term Channeling. This was described in Henry Reed's book, *On Channeling Your Higher Self*, one of the most influential books on Channeling available today. Cayce believed that the body had a direct path that connected with the Universe. He believed that, if you are made in the image and likeness of God, then you have a direct connection to the Divine.

CREATING SPACE FOR REFLECTION—Consider the word "Channel" as its definition of a body of water. When you're on a dock, facing the Channel, that body of water connects you and the Universe; remember that your body is a Channel and you can already access the Universe. Allow yourself to begin to start the conversation and connect because the Mothership is waiting.

MOVING FORWARD—John Mayer sang a song about your body being a wonderland. Divine energy could be described as that wonderland. Stand outside and feel the wind. Feel the energy. Feel the vibrations. Feel the Universe. Now, you're talking.

Will Your Unspoken Dream Become a Reality?

Everybody has one . . . an unspoken dream. You cannot deny it, and I cannot deny it. Deep within our soul, in that place that perhaps no one except for God, the Universe, and Spirit knows, lays our unspoken dream.

The dream lays there, dormant, waiting for that spark of interest, that thought, that light to be awakened. Once awake, the dream starts to take form and become a reality.

Unfortunately, the majority of dreams remain asleep and never see the light of day.

The folks that I've had the pleasure of giving readings to have been receptive to Spirit bringing their dreams to the surface in order to see the light.

When I bring forth the dreams that only they knew about, and that Spirit wants them to explore and seriously contemplate, the looks and smiles on their faces are the most satisfying rewards of developing my gifts.

I have also been on the receiving end of a reading, and have been told about dreams that only I knew. It's hard to deny that it's an awesome feeling. Thank the Universe for that feeling.

Time to give that dream that you've had for the longest time some attention, some oxygen. Let it breathe . . . let it come to life. Send your thoughts and verbalize the dream to the Universe, for it to become a reality.

NAVIGATING THE MESSAGE—Open that store, start that business, go back to school, take that class, start that path of ministry, get your body the way you want it to be, go for that promotion, change your career, change your course . . . change your life. In the process, you will change the lives of people around you for the better.

CREATING SPACE FOR REFLECTION—People say zombies don't really exist, but, at times in our lives, don't we feel like zombies? You go through routine after routine after routine, day in and day out. In high school or in college or when you were young, is this what you thought your life was going to be like? Is this what you signed up for? If not, then consider a change in your life.

MOVING FORWARD—And while you're looking at making a big change in your life, don't forget to help others achieve their dreams, as well. One of our main purposes in life is to help people find their lives. Here's to our dreams and to making them a reality.

A Distant Shore Isn't So Distant, Once You Make the Effort

When I first started using my gifts as a psychic, medium, and clairvoyant, I felt like something was holding me back. I felt like there was a wall that I just couldn't push through. The readings that I was privileged enough to give people seemed to be working, but I needed more education, information, and experience so that I had the full confidence and experience to deliver the messages–or so I thought. My soul was telling me not to "reach across the aisle" and meet the Universe halfway for a compromise on my gifts. My soul was telling me to "go the distance," (see the movie *Field of Dreams*[6]) and, whatever I did, don't stop halfway.

Whether it's physical, spiritual, emotional, mental, etc., sometimes the distance in our lives isn't what keeps us apart. It's not realizing that there is a distance between us and our goals, dreams, aspirations, and gifts. Sometimes it's ignorance that is hindering our efforts, not knowing what the full impact on our lives would be if we made the effort to "get to the other side," to push a little bit further to see what is out there, to see what borders exist within us that keep us from realizing our full potential as citizens of the Universe. Or it's just plain laziness, and we simply don't want to waste our time and energy doing something that may not pay off. After all, we may have the attitude to say, think or feel, that it's just not worth it.

On a daily basis, our intuition tells us to make the effort, to take the first step and not to be afraid to close the gap on anything that we view as unreachable and distant in our lives.

Our intuition, which is our soul and the Universe talking to us, tells us that there is more to life than what we're currently experiencing.

Unfortunately, on a daily basis, we dismiss that intuition or that voice inside us that says we must reach across the boundaries that keep us on our own side. We say to our self, "Not today," or, "Too busy," or, "Why don't they reach out to me? Why does it always have to be me?"

Yet, we refuse to come out of our bomb shelter even after hearing the all-clear siren. Why is that?

Is it because society tells us that structure is more important than imagination?

Is it because boundaries are more important than freedom? Is it because, by playing it safe, no one will get hurt and everything will be normal or back to normal?

I've got to admit that my gifts have alienated a few people in my life who felt I was dabbling in new age spirituality, or doing the work of the dark side, or not being faithful to my Catholic religion, etc.

I had to push through boundaries and borders in order to reach the distant shores of my gifts in order to use them to help people on their journey. And I haven't looked back since.

I've discovered gifts that God has given me. Intuition tells me to listen to the voices in my head, to pay attention to what the Universe is showing me, and to heed what God is telling me.

Psychic, medium, clairvoyant . . . these are the gifts that intuition continues to push me to develop in order to help people. That's my distant shore which isn't distant anymore.

NAVIGATING THE MESSAGE—So what is on your distant shore? Is it forgiveness from yourself? Are there people that you have hurt that you're afraid won't forgive you? Have there been signs in your life that you're ignoring or missing? If it's forgiveness, then there cannot be a greater shore to reach.

CREATING SPACE FOR REFLECTION—Is there something blocking you from living your life to the fullest? Has someone told you not to go for that distant shore because it's too far?

Because it's "just not what you need to be doing?" Because that distant shore is meant for other people and not you? Now, look over the horizon; what do you see in the distance that you long to do? Long to discover? Long to be?

MOVING FORWARD—Is there something keeping you from moving forward to reach that shore? Chances are that there is much on that distant shore that you have been neglecting far too long. It's time to reach for the shore because, in reality, it's closer than you think.

When a Candle Is Lit, the Lost Begin to Find Their Way

To me, candles are one of the pathways to the Universe. Light attracts light, and the brighter the light, the brighter the pathway. The brighter the light, the more it attracts Spirit from the higher side of life, and that's what we desire. Spirit from the higher side of life will only come for our best and highest good, so lit candles–preferably white candles–please the Universe greatly.

Before every reading, I light a candle in honor of God, the Universe, Spirit, my Spirit Guides and helpers, and also for my ancestors who have gone before me. Candles serve multiple purposes here on Earth, but they also serve multiple purposes in the Spirit world, as well.

A few years ago, a friend of mine took his own life. We were all devastated when we heard the news.

He was way too young, and had so much potential left on this Earth plane. So sad, too, because he was a man of the cloth.

In my weekly meditation circle, it was revealed that my friend, whom we will call "D," was on the other side, but he was lost; he could not find his way.

Spirit told us that we needed to light a candle to help him find the way to the light.

With my two best friends in my Saturday-morning prayer group, we sat around a candle, closed our eyes, and prayed. Before the prayer was over, Spirit whispered to me, "The candle is extinguished . . . he has found his way."

Coming out of prayer, we opened our eyes, and the candle was indeed out. D had found the light. With just a flicker of a flame, a soul had gone home.

NAVIGATING THE MESSAGE—At some point or another in our lives, we all need to find our way home.

CREATING SPACE FOR REFLECTION—Candles are powerful beacons to the Universe. Here or in the Spirit world, someone is always lost and needs to find their way to the light. Light attracts light, and this is a very good thing.

MOVING FORWARD—Tonight, find time to light a candle and say a prayer for the lost, whether they are here or in the Spirit world. Tonight, someone might be lighting a candle for you.

---

1. Pg. 88 - Awtry, M. Author, Lecturer, Clairvoyant.
2. Pg. 93 - Jung, C. Swiss Psychiatrist, Psychoanalyst.
3. Pg. 94 - Mayer, J. (2002). Your Body Is a Wonderland. Columbia Records.
4. Pg. 94 - Reed, H. (1989). *Edgar Cayce on Channeling Your Higher Self.* Grand Central Publishing, p.14.
5. Pg. 95- Reed, H. (1989). *Edgar Cayce on Channeling Your Higher Self.* Grand Central Publishing, p.14.
6. Pg. 98 - *Field of Dreams.* (1989). Directed by P. Robinson. Universal Pictures.

Chapter 7

GRACE

Have You Ever Been Exiled?

One of the most liberating things I've experienced while giving readings is truly helping people on their path with their fears and doubts. One of those fears that often pops up is being alone. At times, it's almost an epidemic.

Being alone is one of the most frightening feelings and thoughts that we possess.

Being left alone, left out, forgotten, abandoned, left for dead, exiled. The feeling that no one cares, no one reaches out to you, no one returns your call. Silence and darkness. No friends or family to throw you a lifeline.

When imagining ourselves in the vastness of the Universe, one could easily feel alone.

A horrible feeling . . . or is it? What's so wrong about being left out? After all, what's so wrong about not fitting in? What's so wrong about not going along with the masses? What's so wrong about being alone? To some, it is the worst fear imaginable; but are you really alone?

We are forced somewhat to think about our lives, about what we are and what we want to become, and, more importantly, what we have been called to do.

In the darkness, sometimes, is when we encounter our Higher Self . . . that part of us deep within our consciousness that directly connects with the Spirit realm.

Being alone, up to a point, can lead to independence, where you stand up for what you believe, for who you are and for who you want to be.

Independence is a beautiful thing . . . a liberating thing.

If others exiled you, it is their loss and your gain.

It is a win for you in terms of getting to know yourself better. Let's face it, you can't do that in the middle of a crowd. I have given readings to folks who truly feel they have no one or nowhere to turn to. They feel like they want to hide, but they can't. But the message that comes through, time and time again, is that it's okay. It's okay to feel this way, and the Universe understands this. You are beyond significant to the Universe, and you will always be a part of something bigger than yourself.

NAVIGATING THE MESSAGE—It's okay to be alone, and it's okay to feel like you're all by yourself because Spirit and the Universe are always with you.

CREATING SPACE FOR REFLECTION—When we're alone, we can feel the vibrations that the Universe wants us to feel. We can hear what the Universe wants us to hear. And we can start to discern our true mission in life. Just remember that eventually you have to come out of isolation and rejoin society. You have people to meet and help on their paths and places to go where you've never been. You have experiences in life that await you.

MOVING FORWARD—What's the downside of being exiled? The answer is up to you. Being exiled can truly be an uplifting experience, so try being alone for a time; you might be surprised by how much you will look forward to the next time.

Are You a Mirror Image of Yourself?

Let's face it, we're curious creatures. We want to know about our finance, health, relationships, education, career, friendships, family, etc. What our neighbors are doing, and what their kids are doing, and when will we go to the moon again, and what does retirement look like, and what church should we go to, and when will our kids get married, etc. We wake up every morning with questions on our mind and go to bed sometimes with the very same questions that started the day. The list is as endless as our thirst for knowledge and our never-ending quest to simply know what is going on in our lives, our kids' lives, our neighborhood, our city, our state, our world, etc. And that's okay, for God made us thirst for knowledge and ask questions about these things and more.

So, when do we ask questions to ourselves, about ourselves? When do we ask ourselves about what we want in life? Not what people or society tells us what we should want or have, but deep inside, what we really want out of life.

People come to me for readings and, for that, I'm truly grateful and appreciative. But what I often tell people is that they don't need me to tell them what they should be doing in their lives. Deep down, they already know what they should be doing, but they will never know unless they start taking a good look at themselves and ask themselves questions about life and their purpose in life.

Believe it or not, a good way to look at yourself more deeply is to look in a mirror. Mirrors are everywhere we look. Mirrors remind us of not only how we look, but also how we want to look. Mirrors tell us that we are beautiful, that we are accepted, that we are just as good as anyone else. Mirrors remind us also of the pain, the scars, the wrinkles, and lines that define our years on this Earth plane. The scars, the pain, the anguish, the hurt, and the disappointments are all told on our faces.

What if you could look in the mirror and not see those things on the surface, but instead see deep inside? What if you could look in a mirror and ask yourself honest questions about yourself, without getting distracted by your image in the mirror? You can, and all it takes is one little exercise . . . here it is.

Go and sit in front of a big mirror and take a look at yourself. Now turn off all of the lights, so that it is so dark you cannot see yourself in the mirror. What do you see? You know your image is there, but it's just not that important anymore because you cannot see it. Your reflection is there, but it is not visible. Your image is there but the eyes do not make it out.

Sit for about five minutes in total darkness and keep looking at the mirror. What do you feel? What do you hear? What is it that you want to ask yourself?

By not focusing on your image, you are free to ask yourself questions about your life with no distractions. I wonder what it is you will ask yourself?

NAVIGATING THE MESSAGE—There are questions in the darkness. There are also answers if you sit long enough.

CREATING SPACE FOR REFLECTION—Images can be distracting, and, when we no longer look at ourselves in the mirror, we tend to look deep within. That's where the real beauty is; that's where the soul is, and that's where the answers to your questions are.

MOVING FORWARD—Turn the lights out and take a look in the mirror. Say hello to yourself. The time for introductions is long overdue.

I See a Heart in the Shape of a Dog Tag

I'm an analytical person, and that, in and of itself, carries a significant challenge when it comes to matters of the heart or of a spiritual nature. I have to analyze everything, and, if it doesn't fit just right, it frustrates the heck out of me. If you're like me, I know you'll appreciate where I'm coming from. So to give messages and readings from "dead" people, and from people who are hundreds of years old (Spirit Guides), and from the Universe itself leaves an analytical person like myself a bit unsure of . . . well . . . everything.

I'm one of the world's biggest skeptics, and I push back on things when I cannot connect the dots. Until, one night, when I stepped out and took a leap of faith.

I had been in a weekly meditation circle with about a dozen or so mediums for a couple of years and was told it was time for me to do Spirit's work.

The circle was a classroom of sorts for me to develop my gifts from God; but I sat on the sidelines until that night, when, in the middle of the circle, I was told that Spirit wanted me to get up and give a message to the person across from me.

I was petrified . . . after all, what if I don't get anything? And even if I do, what if I get the message(s) wrong? What if I make a fool out of myself in front of all of these people? What if I let Spirit down? God down? The Universe down?

Never mind that earlier, in the day, while on a walk, I envisioned myself giving a message in the circle. Spirit was preparing me for what was to come.

Back in the circle, it was time for me to start to realize my purpose in life. I slowly got up and went to the middle of the circle, and with my eyes closed and straining to see past the darkness, came the following awe-inspiring words out of my mouth, "I see a heart . . . but it's in the shape of a dog tag."

What? That's it? C'mon, God . . . no more than that? Universe, where are you now that I need you? What the heck is going on, O' great and wise Spirit?

It was quiet for a minute or so, and then the lady across from me spoke.

"We were just told that my dog has a heart condition; your message was spot on." Universe hadn't let me down . . . I had. My lack of confidence in what Spirit was showing me and telling me was preventing me from giving messages to people and helping them on their path in life.

You see, I thought that it was my gift to interpret all of the messages that I was given to the person in front of me. Remember, I'm analytical, and that mindset of having to connect all the dots and put everything together doesn't really work in the grand scheme of things as far as the Universe is concerned.

I learned many a lesson that night. I don't have to analyze everything that I'm given. I don't have to connect the dots for everyone and everything. I don't have to explain every little detail the way that I see it. None of that is important. None of that matters.

NAVIGATING THE MESSAGE—The Universe doesn't connect the dots. The Universe doesn't adhere to any one system or any one order. Its order IS chaos, and evolution, and movement because that's how life is and that's how our soul is.

CREATING SPACE FOR REFLECTION—The Universe is the ultimate non-conformist. The Universe is the ultimate rebel. A rebel takes leaps of faith, makes decisions, and then stands by those decisions.

MOVING FORWARD—What chance will you take? What leap of faith are you willing to take? Are you with us? Time to join the revolution.

It's Time to Schedule Your Meltdown

Anger is an emotion that normally doesn't come out of the readings that I do. But there have been times that I could feel and sense deep, within the person in front of me, something simmering that soon would reach a boiling point. Trust me, I've been plenty angry in my life about any number of things, so I'm not immune to this emotion. But what was simmering wasn't anger so much as bitterness, and that's a horse of another color. To me, that is something far worse. To be angry is, for the most part, temporary, or at least should be. Bitterness, however, lingers much longer and leaves deeper scars.

Anger is the train that arrived at the station five minutes late, and bitterness is the train that leaves the station two days later. Bitterness is the result of anger not being respected. So, I believe we should have more meltdowns.

It is amazing that, with everything going on around us, through us, and in us, we do not have more meltdowns! The ability to let go and just lose it is a lost art . . . an art that needs to be recaptured and shared with all of the world.

In the movie, *Network,* there comes an iconic moment when the late, great Peter Finch, as a TV anchor, implores his audience to go to their windows and shout, "I'm mad as hell, and I can't take it anymore!"[1] (or something to that effect).

This is EXACTLY how we feel . . . broken relationships; kids that are sick and possibly dying; stress at work; neighbors that aren't neighborly; cars break down; money's not there to repair the washing machine . . . the list is endless.

Some of the people that I've had the pleasure to give readings to need to spend time in the darkness. They need to release the negative energy and send it out to the Universe. They need to yell and scream and let it out. They need to absolutely go for broke and go through every human emotion there is.

Just look at the seven basic human emotions:

- ANGER
- SADNESS
- SURPRISE
- CONTEMPT
- JOY
- FEAR
- DISGUST

The overwhelming majority of the human emotions are not very complimentary . . . perfect ingredients for a meltdown. If meltdowns do not happen and anger is not allowed to be let out, then bitterness will simmer beneath the surface and fester. Trust me, bitterness will take down more people than anger ever thought about. Let the meltdown shake you to your core, and you won't be sorry.

NAVIGATING THE MESSAGE—Find an outlet to have that meltdown, but, unlike previous messages in this book that instruct you to take people along to help them on their journey, this is a journey you must travel alone. On the meltdown journey, you need to go to the deepest part of your soul in order to learn more about yourself and to see why anger is still hanging around. I know of only one way to prevent bitterness from setting up residence in your soul and that's to let the anger out in some form or fashion. Me? I used to go hit tennis balls against a big outside wall . . . that was my release.

Now's the time to find your release.

CREATING SPACE FOR REFLECTION—Pick and choose the time to have these meltdowns because, in todays' world, you've more than earned it.

It's time for you to have that meltdown that you have promised yourself. You do not need permission or even an audience.

MOVING FORWARD—Spend a few minutes in darkness and take a look at what is making you angry. You will learn that the Universe is there to help you back on your path. But in the meantime, go ahead and have a meltdown . . . the Universe is waiting to watch the show.

With Every Breath, Are We Living or Dying?

In *The Shawshank Redemption*, there is a line that says, "Get busy living, or get busy dying,"[2] which seems to be one of the major points of the movie.

It can also serve as a theme for our lives . . . what will our choice be when it comes to our time here on this Earth plane?

Breathing is something we do every second of every day; but with each breath, do we draw closer to living out our purpose and mission in life, or do we just assume that we're one step closer to death?

Living out our purpose and mission in life takes all we have, but do we feel like pursuing that dream? That purpose? That mission? The Universe wants us to get busy living and moving forward.

Some people just feel like every day is one day closer to the end, whereas other people feel like every day is a second chance . . . a chance to learn from the mistakes of the past and move on to a higher, more enriched life. So, what do you think God wants you to do?

It's no accident that most meditations and most spiritual exercises begin with being aware of our breathing and slowing down . . . slow . . . slow . . . slow.

I love it when it's cold, and even though it doesn't get too cold in Florida where I live, I do travel a lot, and I'm absolutely thrilled when I get to go into a cold climate. I love seeing my breath because it's a reminder of how precious breathing is and how precious life is.

NAVIGATING THE MESSAGE—The Universe is talking to you through your breath, and it's tough to listen with so much noise around you.

CREATING SPACE FOR REFLECTION—Ask yourself this question . . . am I living the life I was meant to live?

MOVING FORWARD—In the next day or so, slow down for a few minutes, notice your breathing, and take note of everything around you.

Breathing is life, and life is worth living every day.

The Story of the Person Behind You

Before I do a reading, I say a prayer, offer up protection during the reading, and ask that our Spirit Guides and the Universe offer up any messages or guidance for the person(s) receiving the reading. I never know in advance what story or stories the Universe will decide to share. This sharing will help the person with their path in life.

We all have to wait in lines. Whether we're in line at a store, or in a drive-through, or one of the many lines in which we find ourselves on a day-to-day basis, there are always people behind us.

Have you ever wondered what is going on in that car? Or what is going on with the person in line behind you? What's their story?

What does your intuition tell you? Are they dealing with a loss? Are they dealing with some sort of tragedy? Depression? Financial stress? Addiction? Suicide? On the other hand, are they just one good deed away from having an awesome day? Would a small pick-me-up be just the thing that they need? Maybe all they need is to see or experience first-hand a random act of kindness, so they can pass it on. The list could be endless.

Every now and then I will buy the coffee for the car behind me in line at Starbucks, and, most of the time, it costs less than eight dollars. Eight dollars to start someone's day off the right way.

I never hang around for them to thank me. I just hang around to see the amazing smile that suddenly appears on their face.

One day I was informed by the Starbucks associate in the drive thru window that I started a nine-car chain reaction of each car buying the coffee for the car behind them. I've been on the receiving end of these chains, too, and those have been the times that I really needed something uplifting that day.

NAVIGATING THE MESSAGE—There's no telling what a little course correction will do for someone's state of mind.

CREATING SPACE FOR REFLECTION—We all have issues that we have to deal with . . . chances are, once we see everyone else's issues, we wouldn't trade ours for theirs in a million years. Let's take time today to reflect and thank God for our issues.

MOVING FORWARD—Next time you're in a line, say a little prayer for the person behind you. Send them some love . . . send them some light . . . send them some healing. We all have the ability to do this.

Just ask Spirit to give them some comfort, if only for a day.

At the end of the day, it's only eight dollars. Eight dollars for a million-dollar smile.

Seems worth it to me.

Will Our Final Words Be Our Legacy?

Unfortunately, it's too familiar to most of us. We say something hurtful out of anger to someone, and we never see that person again.

Or the tables are turned . . . someone says something hurtful to us, and then they disappear, or, worse, they pass away and transition to the Spirit world. They're gone.

Words linger and linger and linger, and we can never buy them back once they are uttered.

It's often said that when you get married, you should never go to bed angry. Good luck with that one. At the time I wrote this book, I'd been happily married for over thirty-seven years, and, yes, there were times we went to bed angry at each other. It's called life, and it happens. But the next day, we found a way to have a conversation and keep the dialogue going.

It isn't easy, but we make it work. Keep the conversation going.

There are a couple of things that I absolutely love about the gifts of mediumship/psychic/clairvoyance. When I connect to Spirit, I've witnessed people who have passed, and they are telling the person receiving the reading that they truly are sorry for what they said and what they did, and that the love is still there. Nothing but love.

Final words.

When we leave a meeting or a conversation, there are opportunities for someone to have the last word. If that someone is you, what will you say? What impression will you leave?

Let me give an example.

I was asked to assist with a church retreat and had said yes. Then it happened: a few people had heard about my gifts and were struggling to understand them, to say the least. I was politely asked by the group running the retreat to heavily consider not participating because of what people may say or think of my gifts.

I told the gentlemen that it was okay, that I was all right with withdrawing from the retreat. It was meant to be. I believed it then, and I still do now.

My final words from this conversation could have been angry, or mad, or bitter. But what purpose does that serve?

I wanted my final words from this conversation to give these men comfort that everything was going to be okay. And can't we all use some comfort every now and then?

NAVIGATING THE MESSAGE—Sometimes in life we simply say or do things that we do not mean. We enter a house . . . a room . . . a conversation with good intentions, but leave somewhat bitter for whatever reason, and that's when the pain starts. It starts when we leave, not when we arrive.

CREATING SPACE FOR REFLECTION—There's always going to be pain in life, but we can't let our last words to someone be the legacy that we leave behind in their lives or ours.

MOVING FORWARD—No final words from you, or anyone else for that matter, should come close to bordering on bitterness. Bitterness lingers and eats away at you. It's a poison that slowly spreads and consumes you. Let's watch our words as we walk away; we will never know when it's going to be the last words that someone hears from us. Or . . . from anyone.

---

1. Pg. 111 - *Network.* (1976). Directed by S. Lumet. MGM.
2. Pg. 114 - *The Shawshank Redemption.* (1994). Directed by F. Darabont. Columbia Pictures.

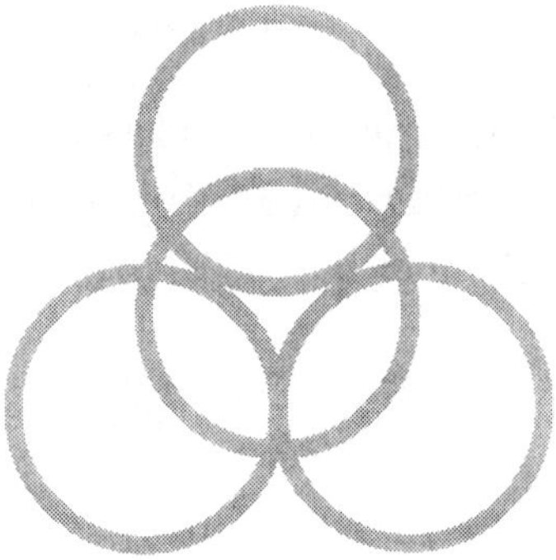

REVIEWS & TESTIMONIALS -READINGS

ENLIGHTENED: Jerry was a pleasure to meet. I felt very comfortable spending time listening to the messages he picked up on, especially the ones from my mom and grandma. Jerry . . . is very in tune . . . he even picked up on my own psychic abilities, which I have no control of, and gave me some messages to help guide me in that area.

I was wowed a few times. What a fun and enlightened experience!

I highly recommend Jerry.

I'll add one more thing. Jerry told me about an Indian drumming behind me who also had a clock . . . turns out my daughter had an Indian drummer with a clock in her dream two nights before my reading!

Jerry said it was a decision I'll have to make soon . . .

V.T.—Orlando

THANKS: Thank you very much for doing my reading.

It made me so very happy . . . you have a very special gift.

Ashley—Illinois

ACCURACY: I want to thank you for the reading . . . you definitely have a gift and glad you are finally using it. I want you to know how accurate you were, as I shared some of our conversation with my son and daughter-in-law.

You mentioned the following . . . two gentlemen; father like figures, one with hat and mustache . . . my daughter-in-law is 100% that this is her grandfather who raised her. He passed away two years ago.

June/July . . . baby/pregnancy . . . my son was shocked to hear this because they had not shared their timeline with anyone . . . but this is what they both had agreed on.

Many of the other things you mentioned about me and my life were spot on. So happy you are using the gifts that God gave you . . . He calls us in so many ways.

Margie B.—Arizona

IN-DEPTH: Thank you, Jerry, for "seeing me" through your Spirit guides. Hence; I call my reading 'in depth!' You were on point about experiences happening over fifty years ago. You were on point about present happenings and predicted something that would happen just a few hours after I left your zen-like home.

I sometimes question the road I could or should have chosen for my life path, and I must let you know I felt a sense of peace, knowing I have chosen the path God has allowed me!!!

Thank you again and again for my awesome reading!!! God Bless you always and, I pray He continues to inspire you with your life's work!

Anita B.—New Jersey

COMFORTABLE: I enjoyed the reading you provided so very much . . . I felt very at ease and at peace throughout our time together and when we were done. My aunt's nickname for me was something I had not thought of in decades. It brought a smile to my face later that evening when I finally remembered the nickname. You truly have a gift and, I hope that you continue to share it with others.

Andrea B.—Tennessee

CANCER FREE: Your reading was correct . . . both of my tests came back cancer free . . . yippee!!

K.G.—Ft Lauderdale, Florida

AMAZING: You have been blessed with an amazing gift!

Angela R.—Washington

THOUGHT PROVOKING: Thank you, Jerry, for an amazing reading! It was truly insightful, thought provoking, and you hit on so many truths.

Mary H.—Idaho

INSIGHTFUL: Great experience, and I thank you for the emotional and insightful reading that you gave me.

F.W.—West Palm Beach, Florida

MIRACULOUS: Received my miracles today. I asked the Universe, and I was heard. Congratulations and proud of you.

L.D.—South Florida

AMAZING: Great talking to you. You are amazing. I can't wait to do a reading with you.

D.S.—Florida

SPOT ON: Jerry is the real deal! He told me things that are currently happening in my life that he didn't know about and was spot on! He has a beautiful gift and is using it to his fullest potential! I left with a peaceful heart and mind after his reading!

S.S.—Orlando

AUTHENTIC: Jerry is the real deal. He is gifted, and his sessions are generous-chock full of value. I found the information that he has access to was indeed accurate, very relevant, very helpful, and his style is authentically humble. He creates a safe environment that welcomes your curiosity and interaction-both safe and sacred. I encourage you-if you are curious, book a session with Jerry!

L.B.—Florida

For psychic, medium, and clairvoyant readings, please contact . . .

Jerry P. McDaniel

Individual & Group Readings Available
In Person, by Phone and Skype
Phone: 407-718-9903
Email: jmacmedium@gmail.com
Twitter: @Jmacmedium
Website: www.jmacmedium.com

NOTES FROM THE MOTHERSHIP

Chapter 1 - Enlightenment

NOTES FROM THE MOTHERSHIP

Chapter 1 - Enlightenment

NOTES FROM THE MOTHERSHIP

Chapter 2 - Courage

NOTES FROM THE MOTHERSHIP

Chapter 2 - Courage

NOTES FROM THE MOTHERSHIP

Chapter 3 - Wisdom

NOTES FROM THE MOTHERSHIP

Chapter 3 - Wisdom

NOTES FROM THE MOTHERSHIP

Chapter 4 - Silence

NOTES FROM THE MOTHERSHIP

Chapter 4 - Silence

NOTES FROM THE MOTHERSHIP

Chapter 5 - Discovery

NOTES FROM THE MOTHERSHIP

Chapter 5 - Discovery

NOTES FROM THE MOTHERSHIP

Chapter 6 - Hope

NOTES FROM THE MOTHERSHIP

Chapter 6 - Hope

NOTES FROM THE MOTHERSHIP

Chapter 7 - Grace

NOTES FROM THE MOTHERSHIP

Chapter 7 - Grace

ABOUT THE AUTHOR

Jerry McDaniel had a career in sales, management, marketing, and training for over thirty years. During this time, he assisted in training over three thousand sales associates, managers, vice presidents, and customers from some of the largest retail chains in the U.S.. He has also helped to put on Catholic leadership retreats for men and has been a leader in the Cursillo movement in the Central Florida Diocese.

However, he felt there was more to life than what he was doing. He knew there was another calling for him to fulfill. Little did he know that the calling was coming from within him, and a chance encounter with a medium that was cleaning his house put him on the path that he is on today. He started to explore his metaphysical gifts from a spiritual point of view, and after some time sitting in a weekly mediumship circle, he started to give messages and readings to friends, family members, co-workers, and strangers from all walks of life.

These readings consisted of loved ones coming through to deliver messages, psychic visions of things that have yet to come, and clairvoyant information about the past, present, and future.

Today, he is a certified psychic, medium, and clairvoyant and his readings, messages and writings have interacted with thousands of people in over forty five countries. He has completed additional courses in Spiritualism, Natural Law, and Mediumship, as well as a course in Metaphysics.

Then, Jerry started to write about spiritual and metaphysical matters. He was directed by God, Spirit, and the Universe to take his writings, messages, and readings from a two-year period and put them into a book. *Channeling the Mothership: Messages from the Universe* is his first book, in which Jerry seeks to share wisdom and techniques for readers to begin channeling their Universe and Spirit.

Jerry continues to give messages and readings to people from all over the world and is currently working on his second book.

CPSIA information can be obtained
at www.ICGtesting.com
Printed in the USA
FFOW02n0100180917
40034FF

9 780998 826103